D1642213

LUDWIG WITTGENSTEIN

LETTERS TO RUSSELL,
KEYNES AND MOORE

LUDWIG WITTGENSTEIN

LETTERS TO RUSSELL KEYNES AND MOORE

Edited with an Introduction by

G. H. von Wright

assisted by B. F. McGuinness

BASIL BLACKWELL · OXFORD

ISBN 0 631 15180 X

Library of Congress Catalog Card Number
73–86009

Printed in Great Britain by
William Clowes & Sons, Limited
London, Becccles and Colchester
and bound by Kemp Hall Bindery, Oxford

CONTENTS

CONTENTS

INTRODUCTION

WITTGENSTEIN first came to see Russell at Cambridge on 18 October, 1911.[1] He was, however, still registered as present in the University of Manchester in the autumn of that year. On 1 February 1912 he was admitted a member of Trinity College, Cambridge. His status seems first to have been that of an undergraduate. In the beginning of June the Degree Committee of the Special Board for Moral Science admitted him as an Advanced Student to a Course of Research and "asked Mr. Bertrand Russell to be kind enough to act as the Director and Supervisor of the Student".[2]

Wittgenstein was in residence at Trinity during all three terms in the year 1912 and during the Lent and Easter Terms of 1913. The greater part of the academic year 1913–1914 he was in Norway. In April G. E. Moore came to see him there. In August 1914, immediately after the outbreak of the war, Wittgenstein volunteered for the Austrian army. After its surrender in November 1918 he was a prisoner of war, for the most part at Cassino in southern Italy, until August of the following year. He had with him the completed typescript of his early work, the *Tractatus*. He was able to send it to Russell from the prison camp through the intermediacy of another of his friends from Cambridge, John Maynard Keynes.

Fifty-seven letters from Wittgenstein to Bertrand Russell have

---

[1] Letter from Russell to Lady Ottoline Morrell of 18 October 1911. There are several references to Wittgenstein in Russell's letters to Lady Ottoline from this time on and until after the first World War. I am indebted to Mr Kenneth Blackwell of the Bertrand Russell Archives at McMaster University for information concerning this correspondence, which is located in the Humanities Research Center, University of Texas.

[2] Letter of 5 June 1912 from J. N. Keynes, University Registrary, to Dr W. M. Fletcher, Tutor at Trinity College.

been preserved, fifty-seven letters or other communications to
G. E. Moore, and thirty-one to Keynes. Of overwhelming interest are the letters to Russell. With the exception of four all come
from the period 1912–1921, between the early germination and
the final publication of the *Tractatus*. In 1922 Wittgenstein and
Russell met at Innsbruck. The meeting led to a rupture in their
friendship, which was never restored to what it had been before.

   Wittgenstein's withdrawal from philosophy to become a
teacher in elementary schools in remote villages in the Austrian
countryside (1920–1926) did not mean a complete breach of relations with Cambridge. Early in 1923 he wrote to Keynes seeking
renewed contact (K.10). The letter remained unanswered for a
whole year. But in September of that same year a young friend of
Keynes's from Cambridge, the brilliant mathematician and philosopher Frank P. Ramsey, who had assisted C. K. Ogden in the
translation of the *Tractatus*, came to see Wittgenstein at Puchberg
am Schneeberg. He seems to have stayed there for at least two
weeks and to have had long daily discussions with Wittgenstein,
who explained the *Tractatus* to him. As a result of these talks a
number of alterations and corrections were made both to the
German text and to the English translation.[1] It must have been
the reports obtained from Ramsey which stirred Keynes to gener-
ous efforts to secure Wittgenstein's return to Cambridge (K.11
and comments). There is evidence that Wittgenstein himself in the
autumn of 1923 was contemplating the possibility of giving up
his job as a teacher and coming to Cambridge to take a degree.
But in the following year he declined Keynes's invitation and explained his reasons both to Keynes and to Ramsey, who was then
again seeing him in Austria. In August 1925, however, Wittgenstein did visit England (Manchester and Cambridge). He received
some financial assistance for the journey from Keynes (K13–14).

   Only one personal letter from Wittgenstein to Ramsey is
known to have been preserved. There is also the beginning of a
draft of a letter, evidently written in 1923 before Ramsey had
come to see him, and a fragment of a letter from 1927. The frag-

[1] See C. Lewy, "A Note on the Text of the *Tractatus*", *Mind* N.S. *76*, 1967.

ment constitutes a short essay on the concept of identity. It was inspired by Ramsey's paper "The Foundations of Mathematics" (1925).[1]

Nine letters or brief communications from Ramsey to Wittgenstein are preserved.[2] Possibly they are all that existed. Wittgenstein used to keep letters of any importance or interest. Several of the letters which he received during the 1920's in Austria he gave for custody to his friend Ludwig Hänsel. It is a fairly safe assumption that the two letters from Moore and the three from Keynes which are known to exist are the only ones from them which Wittgenstein considered worth preserving – perhaps besides some letters, now lost, written before the first World War. It seems to me most unlikely that he himself would have destroyed or thrown away the letters from Russell. He probably deposited them with somebody in Austria. They may now be lost – or they may one day come to light. (*One* single letter is known to exist. It was written during the 1914–18 War but did not reach its destination and was returned to Russell, who handed it to Wittgenstein some time after the war. The letter is printed below on p. 6of.)

Little is known about the circumstances which made Wittgenstein take up philosophy again and go to Cambridge to embark upon a new life.[3] (Cf. K17–20.) On his arrival there early in 1929 he first stayed as Keynes's guest in King's College. On 18 January he was readmitted to Trinity. He kept residence during the Lent and Easter terms and proceeded to the Ph.D. degree on 18 June – the *Tractatus* being accepted as a thesis. He was elected a Fellow of Trinity College under Title B on 5 December 1930. After a prolongation the fellowship eventually expired at the end of the academic year 1935–1936. He was re-elected Professorial Fellow

---

[1] See *Ludwig Wittgenstein und der Wiener Kreis*, ed. by B. F. McGuinness, Suhrkamp Verlag, Frankfurt am Main 1967, p. 189 ff.

[2] Published in Ludwig Wittgenstein, *Letters to C. K. Ogden with Comments on the English Translation of the Tractatus Logico-Philosophicus*, ed. by G. H. von Wright, Basil Blackwell, London, and Routledge & Kegan Paul, London and Boston 1973.

[3] Cf. the account by Herbert Feigl, "The Wiener Kreis in America", *Perspectives in American History*, vol. II, Harvard University Press 1968, p. 639.

in October 1939. He resigned his fellowship and his chair as from
31 December 1947.

It is a coincidence worth recording that when Wittgenstein returned to Cambridge at the beginning of 1929, G. E. Moore happened to be on the same train with him from London. Their
friendship had experienced a crisis soon after Moore's visit to
Norway in 1914 (M.8–9) and there had apparently been no contact at all between them in the fifteen intermediate years. From the
time of Wittgenstein's return to Cambridge their friendship was
renewed and remained unbroken to Wittgenstein's death. Wittgenstein's letters bear witness to the deep affection and respect he
had for G. E. Moore in spite of the fundamental dissimilarity of
the two men's personality and thinking.

The letters to Moore and to Keynes (with the exception of a
part of one letter) are in English. Of the letters to Russell twenty-
six are in German. They are here printed with an English translation by Mr Brian McGuinness.

Wittgenstein's English of the earlier years was not always idio-
matic and his spelling, whether English or German, was never
entirely sure. The editor's policy has been not to interfere with
grammar and idiom at all. The English orthography and occasionally also the punctuation, has been corrected without indication. So also the German orthography, when it was obviously
erroneous. Words, or parts of words, in square brackets are the
editor's insertions.

A characteristic of Wittgenstein's style is his use of underlinings
to give emphasis to words and phrases. Words once underlined
are here printed in *italics*; words twice underlined in small capitals; words thrice underlined in big capitals; and words four
times underlined in big capitals with an underlining.

The editor's comments have been restricted, on the whole, to
brief explanations of names or events to which the letters make
reference and which cannot be assumed to be known to the reader. Names, mostly of philosophers, who should be well known to

people familiar with Wittgenstein's work and professional environment, are not explained.

A few letters – mostly quite brief communications – have been omitted on the ground that they neither reveal any biographically relevant data nor concern Wittgenstein's work. The omitted letters too have been assigned a number, however. This explains the occasional gaps in the numbering of the printed letters.

My thanks are due, especially to the late Lord Russell, Mrs Dorothy Moore, and the Librarian of King's College, Cambridge, Dr Munby, for letting me have copies of Wittgenstein's letters; to Dr Hermann Hänsel for copies of letters to Wittgenstein from Keynes and Ramsey; to Sir Geoffrey Keynes for permission to print four letters by J. M. Keynes; to Mrs Lettice Ramsey for permission to print and quote from F. P. Ramsey's letters; to the Editorial Committee of the Bertrand Russell Archives McMaster University for permission to print the one existing letter from Russell to Wittgenstein and to quote from M. H. Dziewicki's letter to Russell about Wittgenstein and from one of Russell's letters to Lady Ottoline Morrell; to Mr Kenneth Blackwell of the Bertrand Russell Archives for several items of information and for helpful comments on the entire edited text; and to Dr W. Methlagl for checking the edited text of the German letters. My greatest debt is to Mr Brian F. McGuinness who, in addition to translating the German letters into English, examined critically the entire text of the edition and contributed many items of information and valuable suggestions.

GEORG HENRIK VON WRIGHT

Letters to Bertrand Russell

1912–1935

4 Rose Cr.
Tuesday 1 a: m

Dear Mr Russell,
I feel very much
tempted to write
to you although
I have very little
to say. I have just
been reading a part
of Moore's Principia
Ethica: (now please don't
be shocked) I do not
like it at all. (Mind

R.3   1.7.12.

DEAR RUSSELL,

Thank you **very** much for your kind letter.

Will you think that I have gone mad if I make the following suggestion?: The sign $(x).\varphi x$ is not a complete symbol but has meaning only in an inference of the kind: from $\vdash \varphi x \supset_x \psi x . \varphi(a)$ follows ψa. Or more generally: from $\vdash(x).\varphi x.\varepsilon_0(a)$ follows $\varphi(a)$. I am – of course – most uncertain about the matter but something of the sort might really be true. I am sorry I cannot spend as much time on thinking about this stuff as I would like to because I have to write a *most* absurd paper on rhythms for the psychological meeting on the 13th. – I hear just now that a sister of mine is going to visit me here on the 6th. Would you mind me introducing her to you? She ought to see everything worth seeing!

Yours most, etc.

LUDWIG WITTGENSTEIN

Letter dated by Russell.

R.1   4 Rose Cr[escent, Cambridge]
                                           Tuesday 1 *a*:m
                                           [Probably June 1912]

DEAR MR RUSSELL,

I feel very much tempted to write to you although I have very little to say. I have just been reading a part of Moore's Principia Ethica: (now please don't be shocked) I do not like it at all. (Mind you, quite *apart* from disagreeing with most of it.) I don't believe – or rather I am sure – that it cannot dream of comparing with Frege's or your own works (except perhaps some of the Phil[osophical] Essays). Moore repeats himself dozens of times, what he says in 3 pages could – I believe – easily be expressed in half a page. *Unclear* statements don't get a bit clearer by being repeated!! – The concert of the 7th of June was most gorgeous! I wish you had heard it. I need not say that I miss you awfully and that I wish I knew how you are and that I am

Yours most, etc.

LUDWIG WITTGENSTEIN

P.S. My logic is all in the melting-pot.

R.*2*   Cambridge 22.6.12.

DEAR RUSSELL,

There are yet some nice events happening in one's life e.g. getting a letter from you (thanks *very* much for it). Much less nice is the following event: I had a discussion with Myers about the relations between Logic and Psychology. I was very candid and I am sure he thinks that I am the most arrogant devil who ever lived. Poor Mrs Myers who was also present got – I think – quite wild about me. However, I think he was a bit less confused after the discussion than before. – Whenever I have time I now read James's "Varieties of religious exp[erience]". This book does me a *lot* of good. I don't mean to say that I will be a saint soon, but I am not sure that it does not improve me a little in a way in which I would like to improve *very much*: namely I think that it helps me to get rid of the *Sorge* (in the sense in which Goethe used the word in the 2nd part of Faust). Logic is still in the melting-pot but one thing gets more and more obvious to me: The prop[osition]s of Logic contain ONLY APPARENT variables and whatever may turn out to be the proper explanation of apparent variables, its consequence *must* be that there are NO *logical* constants.

Logic must turn out to be of a TOTALLY different kind than any other science.

The piece of poetry which you sent me is *most* splendid! DO come to Cambridge soon.

Yours most, etc.

LUDWIG WITTGENSTEIN

I am staying here till about the 20th of July.

Myers. – Charles Samuel Myers (1873–1946) taught psychology at Cambridge and founded the psychological laboratory there in 1912. One of Myers's special interests was the psychology of music, a topic on which Wittgenstein made some experimental research during his studies at Cambridge. In a letter to Lady Ottoline Morrell, Russell tells

that Wittgenstein, at the opening of the laboratory in May 1913 exhibited an apparatus for psychological investigation of rhythm also R.3 and M.7.

poetry. – Perhaps by Russell, who had in April and May written several poems and showed them to Lady Ottoline.

R.4   Hochreit
                                             Post Hohenberg
                                             N[ieder]-Ö[sterreich]
                                             [Summer 1912]

DEAR RUSSELL,

The above address and this perfectly earthly writing paper will
show you that I am not in hell. In fact I am quite well again and
philosophizing for all I am worth. What troubles me most at
present, is not the apparent-variable-business, but rather the
meaning of " ∨ ", " . ", " ⊃ " etc. This latter problem is – I think –
still more fundamental and, if possible, still less recognized as a
problem. *If* "p ∨ q" means a complex at all – which is quite doubt-
ful – *then*, as far as I can see, one must treat " ∨ " as *part* of a copula, in the way we have talked over before. I have – I believe –
tried all possible ways of solution *under that hypothesis* and found
that if any one will do it *must* be something like this: Let us write
the prop[osition] "from ⊢p and ⊢q follows ⊢r" that way: "i[p; q;
r]". Here "i" is a copula (we may call it inference) which copu-
lates *complexes*. Then "$\varepsilon_1(x, y) . \vee . \varepsilon_1(u, z)$" is to mean:

"$\vdash(\varepsilon_1(x,y), \varepsilon_1(z,u), \beta(x,y,z,u)) . i[\varepsilon_1(x,y); \varepsilon_1(z,u); \beta(x,y,z,u)]$
$\vdash(\varepsilon_1(x,y), \varepsilon_1(z,u), \beta(x,y,z,u)) . i[\sim \varepsilon_1(x,y); \varepsilon_1(z,u); \beta(x,y,z,u)]$
$\vdash(\varepsilon_1(x,y), \varepsilon_1(z,u), \beta(x,y,z,u)) . i[\varepsilon_1(x,y); \sim \varepsilon_1(z,u); \beta(x,y,z,u)]$
$\vdash(\varepsilon_1(x,y), \varepsilon_1(z,u), \beta(x,y,z,u)) . i[\sim \varepsilon_1(x,y); \sim \varepsilon_1(z,u); \beta(x,y,z,u)]$
$\vdash\beta(x, y, z, u)$".

If "p ∨ q" does not mean a complex, then heaven knows what
it means!! –

Now I would like to know how you are and *all* about you! If
you are so good to write to me, please write to the following address:

        L.W. *junior* (please don't forget this)
        bei Paul Wittgenstein
        Oberalm bei Hallein
        Salzburg Austria

We have excellent weather here, such that one can do most

thinking in the open air. There is nothing more wonderful in the world than the *true* problems of Philosophy.

Always yours most, etc.

LUDWIG WITTGENSTEIN

Hochreit. – The estate Hochreit in Lower Austria had belonged to Wittgenstein's father since 1894. The family used to live there during the summer. Later in life too, when he had again settled at Cambridge, Wittgenstein often visited the Hochreit and worked there. A considerable part of his literary *Nachlass* was stored at the Hochreit and discovered after his death.

The dating of the letter is by Russell.

It seems to the editor that there is an error in the symbolic expression for a disjunction. The fourth inference should be "i[$\sim \varepsilon_1$ (x, y); $\sim \varepsilon_1$(z, u); $\sim \beta$(x, y, z, u)]". Also the order of the variables in the *definiendum* should be "ε_1(z, u)".

L.W. junior. – An uncle of Wittgenstein's was also called Ludwig (or Louis).

Paul Wittgenstein. – Another uncle of Ludwig Wittgenstein's. He seems to have been the only one in the family circle who encouraged Ludwig's work in philosophy. In an early version of the Preface to the *Tractatus* Wittgenstein acknowledges his gratitude to his uncle for this.

R.5   Oberalm bei Hallein
                                                       Salzburg
                                                       16.8.12.

DEAR RUSSELL,

Thanks for your letter. I am glad you read the lives of Mozart and Beethoven. These are the actual sons of God. Now as to "p ∨ q", etc.: I have thought that possibility – namely that all our troubles could be overcome by assuming different sorts of Relations of signs to things – over and over and over again! for the last 8 weeks!!! But I have come to the conclusion that this assumption does *not* help us a bit. In fact if you work out ANY such theory – I believe you will see that *it does not even touch our problem*. I have lately seen a new way out (or perhaps not out) of the difficulty. It is too long to be explained here, but I tell you so much that it is based on new forms of propositions. For instance: $\sim(p.q)$, which is to mean "the complex p has the opposite form of q's form". That means that $\sim(p.q)$ holds for instance when p is $\varepsilon_1(a, b)$ and q is $\sim\varepsilon_1(c, d)$. Another instance of the new forms is $\vee(p, q, r)$ which means something like: "The form of the comp[lex] r is composed of the forms of p and q in the way 'or'." That means that $\vee(p, q, r)$ holds for instance when p is $\varepsilon_1(a, b)$, q is $\varepsilon_1(c, d)$ and r is $\varepsilon_1(e, f) \vee \varepsilon_1(g, h)$ etc. etc. The rest I leave to your imagination. All this however seems to me *not half* as important as the fact (if it is one) that the whole problem has become very much clearer to me now than it has ever been before. I wish you were here and I could tell you the whole matter for I cannot write it down; it is MUCH too long! Also the app[arent] var[iable]-business has become by far clearer.

Do write again SOON!

                                        Yours most, etc.

                                        LUDWIG WITTGENSTEIN
                                        I feel like mad.

R.6   [Summer 1912]

DEAR RUSSELL,

   I believe that our problems can be traced down to the *atomic* prop[osition]s. This you will see if you try to explain precisely in what way the Copula in such a prop[osition] has meaning.

   I cannot explain it and I think that as soon as an exact answer to this question is given the problems of " v " and of the app[arent] var[iable] will be brought *very* near their solution if not solved. I therefore now think about "Socrates is human". (Good old Socrates!). My Iceland boat leaves Leith on the 7th and I am going to be in Cambridge and London from the 3rd to the 6th. I wonder if I can see you anywhere in that time? I have just read "Chadschi-Murat" by Tolstoy! Have you ever read it? If not, you ought to for it is *wonderful*. I am awfully sorry you have such beastly weather in England! Come with me to Iceland!

                          Yours most, etc., etc.

                                    L. WITTGENSTEIN

                                                        These two
                          How coy!   amorists
                            "   "   were

   My Iceland boat. – Wittgenstein and his friend David Pinsent left
Leith, the port of Edinburgh, on 7 September 1912 for a journey to
Iceland which lasted four weeks.
                                                  more than
                                                      friends
                                    And good for
                                       them!

R.7   IV. Alleegasse 16
                                                       Wien
                                                       26.12.12.

DEAR RUSSELL,

On arriving here I found my father *very* ill. There is no hope
that he may recover. These circumstances have – I am afraid –
rather lamed my thoughts and I am muddled although I struggle
against it.

I had a long discussion with Frege about our Theory of Symbolism of which, I think, he roughly understood the general outline.
He said he would think the matter over. The complex problem is
now clearer to me and I hope very much that I may solve it. I wish
I knew how you are and what sort of time you are having, and all
about you!

                                    Yours ever most, etc.

                                    LUDWIG WITTGENSTEIN

Alleegasse. – The street in which lay the house belonging to Wittgenstein's parents, a pompous building in 19th century baroque style. The
name of the street was later changed to Argentinierstrasse. It was in this
house that Wittgenstein stored the manuscript writings from the time
of the germination of the *Tractatus* which, on his last visit to Vienna
round the New Year 1950, he ordered to be burnt. (See Editors' Preface to *Notebooks 1914–1916*, Basil Blackwell, Oxford 1961.)

R.*8*   IV. Alleegasse 16
                                                   Wien
                                                   6.1.13.

DEAR RUSSELL,

  I am very sorry not yet to have had a line from you!!! Not that
there was anything in my last letter to you, that wanted answering;
but you might have guessed that I feel von allen guten Geistern
verlassen and that therefore I want a letter from you very neces-
sarily. However – I may not be able to come back to Cambridge
at the beginning of Term, as the illness of my poor father is growing very rapidly.

  The Complex Problem is getting clearer to me every day and I
wish I could write clear enough to let you know what I think of
it. Logic is a very good Invention.

                              Immer der Ihrige

                                   LUDWIG WITTGENSTEIN

von allen guten Geistern verlassen. – abandoned by all good spirits.
Immer der Ihrige. – Yours ever.

R.*9*   IV. Alleegasse 16
                                                    Jan[uary] 1913

DEAR RUSSELL,

   Thanks *very* much for both your kind letters! I cannot yet tell
when I shall be able to come back to Cambridge, as the doctors
are still quite uncertain about the duration of my father's illness.
He has not yet any pains but feels on the whole *very* bad having
constantly high fever. This makes him so apathetic that one cannot do him any good by sitting at his bed, etc. And as this was the
only thing that I could ever do for him, I am now perfectly useless
here. So the time of my staying here depends entirely upon
whether the illness will take so rapid a course that I could not risk
to leave Vienna; or not. I hope I shall be able to decide this in a
week's time and I have told Fletcher so. – I have changed my
views on "atomic" complexes: I now think that Qualities, Relations (like Love), etc. are all copulae! That means I for instance
analyse a subject-predicate prop[osition], say, "Socrates is human"
into "Socrates" and "Something is human" (which I think is not
complex). The reason for this, is a very fundamental one: I think
that there cannot be different Types of things! In other words
whatever can be symbolized by a simple proper name must belong
to one type. And further: every theory of types must be rendered
superfluous by a proper theory of the symbolism: For instance if
I analyse the prop[osition] Socrates is mortal into Socrates, Mortality and $(\exists x, y)\varepsilon_1(x, y)$ I want a theory of types to tell me that
"Mortality is Socrates" is nonsensical, because if I treat "Mortal-
ity" as a proper name (as I did) there is nothing to prevent me to
make the substitution the wrong way round. *But* if I analyse [it]
(as I do now) into Socrates and $(\exists x)x$ is mortal or generally into x
and $(\exists x)\varphi(x)$* it becomes impossible to substitute the wrong way
round, because the two symbols are now of a different *kind* themselves. What I am *most* certain of is not however the correctness of
my present way of analysis, but of the fact that all theory of types
must be done away with by a theory of symbolism showing that
what seem to be *different kinds of things* are symbolised by different

kinds of symbols which *cannot* possibly be substituted in one another's places. I hope I have made this fairly clear!

I was *very* interested to hear your views about matter, although I cannot imagine your way of working from sense-data forward. Mach writes such a horrid style that it makes me nearly sick to read him; however, I am very glad that you think so much of a countryman of mine.

Yours most, etc.

LUDWIG WITTGENSTEIN

*Prop[osition]s which I formerly wrote $\varepsilon_2(a, R, b)$ I now write $R(a, b)$ and analyse them into a, b, and $\underbrace{(\exists x, y)R(x, y)}_{\text{not complex}}$.

Letter dated by Russell.

Fletcher. – Sir Walter Morley Fletcher (1873–1933), Tutor and Fellow of Trinity College. (See Introduction p. 1.)

R.*10*   IV. Alleegasse 16
                                          21.I.13.

DEAR RUSSELL,

My dear father died yesterday in the afternoon. He had the most beautiful death that I can imagine; without the slightest pains and falling asleep like a child! I did not feel sad for a single moment during all the last hours, but most joyful and I think that this death was worth a whole life.

I will leave Vienna on Saturday the 25th and will be in Cambridge either on Sunday night or Monday morning. I long very much to see you again.

Yours ever

LUDWIG WITTGENSTEIN

R.11   IV. Alleegasse 16
                                                    Wien
                                                    25.3.13.
DEAR RUSSELL,

   I can't refrain from writing to you, although I have nothing to
tell you. I am as perfectly sterile as I never was, and I doubt
whether I shall ever again get ideas. Whenever I try to think about
Logic, my thoughts are so vague that nothing ever can crystallize
out. What I feel is the curse of all those who have only half a talent;
it is like a man who leads you along a dark corridor with a light
and just when you are in the middle of it the light goes out and you
are left alone. –

   I suppose you are staying with the Whiteheads at present and
hope you are having a good time. If once you have nothing better
to do, do send me a line letting me know how you are, etc., etc.

                                              L. WITTGENSTEIN

R.*12*   [June 1913]

DEAR RUSSELL,

My mother will stay at the Savoy Hotel. So we shall expect you there on Wednesday about 1-15. By the by, please remember that my mother must not know that I was operated last July (if by any chance the conversation should turn on such topics).

I can now express my objection to your theory of judgment exactly: I believe it is obvious that, from the prop[osition] "A judges that (say) a is in the Rel[ation] R to b", if correctly analysed, the prop[osition] "aRb. ∨ . ~aRb" must follow directly *without the use of any other premiss*. This condition is not fulfilled by your theory.

Yours ever
L.W.

Letter dated by Russell. According to Russell's Appointments Diary for 1912–1913, the lunch was going to be on Wednesday, 18 June.

operated. – An operation for a rupture. Wittgenstein had been exempted from military service because of a rupture. He volunteered, however, for the Austrian army immediately after the outbreak of the war in 1914, and was accepted.

your theory of judgment. – The reference evidently is to a projected work on the theory of knowledge which Russell was then writing. Only the first six chapters were published (in *The Monist*, January 1914– April 1915). See also comment on next letter.

R.*13*   Hochreit
                                                        Post Hohenberg
                                                        N[ieder]-Ö[sterreich]
                                                        22.7.13.

DEAR RUSSELL,

Thanks for your kind letter. My work goes on well; every day my problems get clearer now and I feel rather hopeful. All my progress comes out of the idea that the *indefinables* of Logic are of the general kind (in the same way as the so called *Definitions* of Logic are general) and this again comes from the abolition of the real variable. Perhaps you laugh at me for feeling so sanguine at present; but although I have not solved *one* of my problems I feel very, very much nearer to the solution of them all than I ever felt before.

The weather here is constantly rotten, we have not yet had two fine days in succession. I am very sorry to hear that my objection to your theory of judgment paralyses you. I think it can only be removed by a correct theory of propositions. Let me hear from you soon.

                                                        Yours ever, etc.
                                                        L.W.

paralyses you. – In a 1916 letter to Lady Ottoline Morrell, quoted in his *Autobiography* (vol. II, Allen & Unwin, London 1968, p. 57), Russell wrote: "Do you remember that at the time . . . I wrote a lot of stuff about Theory of Knowledge, which Wittgenstein criticized with the greatest severity? His criticism . . . was an event of first-rate importance in my life, and affected everything I have done since. I saw he was right, and I saw that I could not hope ever again to do fundamental work in philosophy. My impulse was shattered, like a wave dashed to pieces against a breakwater."

Pity the 3rd Earl never accepted L.J.W's request to "Splash" against him!

R.*14*   Hochreit
                                         Post Hohenberg
                                         Nieder-Österreich
                                         Austria
                                         [Probably Summer 1913]

DEAR RUSSELL,

   Would you be so kind as to forward the enclosed letter to Mrs
W., I have forgotten her address. I am afraid there are no logical
news today. The weather here is most abominable, it rains all the
day like mad. Just now a crash of thunder came down and I said
"Hell!", which shews that English swear-words are well in my
bones. I hope I can send you some logical news soon. If you have
nothing better to do *please* let me know how you are, etc.

                                    Yours ever most, etc.

                                         L.W.

Mrs W. – Presumably Mrs Alfred North Whitehead.

R.*15*   Hochreit
                                      Post Hohenberg
                                      N[ieder]-Ö[sterreich]
                                      [Probably Summer 1913]

DEAR RUSSELL,

Your axiom of reducibility is $\vdash:(\exists f):\varphi x \equiv_x f!x$; now is this not all nonsense as this prop[osition] has only then a meaning if we can turn the φ into an *apparent* variable. For if we cannot do so no general laws can ever follow from your axiom. The whole axiom seems to me at present a mere juggling trick. Do let me know if there is more in it. The axiom as you have put it is only a schema and the real Pp ought to be $\vdash:.(\varphi):(\exists f):\varphi(x) \equiv_x f!x$, and where would be the use of that?!

Thanks for your letter. I am working very hard. I look forward VERY much to see you in one of the last days of August because I have lots and lots of things to tell you.

                                      Yours ever, etc.
                                      L.W.

Pp. – Primitive proposition.

R.*16*   5.9.13.

DEAR RUSSELL,

I am sitting here in a little place inside a beautiful fiord and thinking about the beastly theory of types. There are still some *very* difficult problems (and very fundamental ones too) to be solved and I won't begin to write until I have got some sort of a solution for them. However I don't think that will in any way affect the Bipolarity business which still seems to me to be absolutely untangible. Pinsent is an enormous comfort to me here. We have hired a little sailing boat and go about with it on the fiord, or rather Pinsent is doing all the sailing and I sit in the boat and work. Shall I get anything out??! It would be awful if I did not and all my work would be lost. However I am not losing courage and go on thinking. Pray for me!

If you see the Whiteheads please remember me to them. My address for the next 3 weeks shall be: Hotel Öistensjö, Öistensjö. Norway.

If you've nothing better to do, *do* write to me how you are, etc. I very often now have the indescribable feeling as though my work was all sure to be lost entirely in some way or other. But I still hope that this won't come true. Whatever happens don't forget me!

                                    Yours ever most, etc.
                                    L.W.

Öistensjö. – We know from the diary which Wittgenstein's friend David Pinsent kept of their journey to Norway that the place was situated on the Hardangerfjord. (The two travellers had reached it by boat from Bergen.) The place, in all evidence, is one the name of which is (nowadays) spelt *Öystese*. It is likely that the name in 1913 was quite commonly spelt *Öisteso*, but Wittgenstein's own spelling here and in the next letter appears to be in error. I am indebted to Mr Olav Flo, Bergen for information concerning this.

R.*17*   Östensö
                                                          Norway
                                                          20.9.13.

DEAR RUSSELL,

Types are not yet solved but I have had all sorts of ideas which seem to me very fundamental. Now the feeling that I shall have to die before being able to publish them is growing stronger and stronger in me every day and my greatest wish would therefore be to communicate *everything* I have done so far to you, *as soon as possible*. Don't think that I believe that my ideas are very important but I cannot help feeling that they might help people to avoid *some* errors. Or am I mistaken? If so don't take *any notice* of this letter. I have of course no judgment at all as to whether my ideas are worth preserving after my death or not. And perhaps it is ridiculous of me even to consider this question at all. But if this is ridiculous please try to excuse this foolishness of mine because it is not a superficial foolishness but the deepest of which I am capable. I see that the further I get on with this letter the less I dare to come to my Point. But my point is this: I want to ask you to let me meet you *as soon as possible* and give me time enough to give you a survey of the whole field of what I have done up to now and if possible to let me make notes for you *in your presence*. I shall arrive in London on the 1st of Oct[ober] and shall have to be in London again on Oct[ober] 3rd (evening). Otherwise I am not fixed in any way and can meet you wherever you like. My address will be the Grand Hotel. – I know that it may be both arrogant and silly to ask you what I have asked you. But such I am and think of me what you like. I will *always* be yours

                                                          L.W.

notes. – See comments to next letter.

Russell noted on the typescript he had made of this letter: "This letter is endorsed in my handwriting 'Oct. 4, 1 p.m.', so I responded to his appeal." From a letter to Lady Ottoline we know that Wittgenstein came to see Russell at Cambridge already on 2 October.

R.*18*   Nordre Bergenhus Amts Dampskibe, Bergen
                      Dampskibet Kommandör d. 17.10.1913

DEAR RUSSELL,

My address is going to be: L.W. c/o Halvard Draegni, Skjolden, Sogn, Norway. I am not yet there. – *Identity is the very Devil*! Types have got a good deal clearer to me on the journey. Hope you have got typewritten business all right. I saw Whitehead before going and he was charming as usual. Let me hear from you *as soon as possible*; I want it badly! Give my love to everybody who wants it.

Yours as long as there is such a thing as

                                                    L.W.

P.S. I am not as far north as I thought I would be as the Inn I intended to stay at is closed during the winter.

The letter is actually dated 17.9. This must be a slip of the pen for 17.10 (see the next letter).

far north. – I believe it was Wittgenstein's original intention to go to the Lofoten Islands in the far north after his return to Norway from England in October 1913. Instead he went to Skjolden near the innermost part of Sognefjord north of Bergen.

In this and the next three letters there is reference to the "Notes on Logic", published posthumously as an appendix to the *Notebooks 1914–1916*. The composition and history of these notes have puzzled students of Wittgenstein's work and the editors (Anscombe and von Wright) of the *Notebooks*. Thanks to the accessibility of new material in the Bertrand Russell Archives and by a careful comparison of all the sources, Mr Brian McGuinness has succeeded in giving a coherent and convincing picture of the whole matter. The reader is referred to his study "Bertrand Russell and Ludwig Wittgenstein's 'Notes on Logic'" in number 102 (1972) of *Revue Internationale de Philosophie* devoted to Russell's philosophy. The basic facts needed for understanding the references to the Notes in the letters, are as follows:

In the course of the time 2–9 October 1913 Wittgenstein saw Russell at Cambridge and tried to explain to him his ideas. Russell, finding it difficult to grasp and remember what Wittgenstein told him, procured a shorthand writer to whom Wittgenstein dictated a "summary" of his thoughts on logic. Of these dictations, which were probably in English,

Russell had a typescript prepared. This is the typescript to which Wittgenstein refers in this letter (R.18) as "typewritten business" and in the
next letter (R.19) as "the typed stuff". This typescript, with corrections
by Wittgenstein and Russell, is now in the Bertrand Russell Archives
and it contains the misprint ("polarity" for "bi-polarity") referred to
in R.20. In R.19 and R.20, however, Wittgenstein also speaks of a
manuscript and in R.21 he is commenting on questions put to him by
Russell which evidently relate to that manuscript and also quoting
from it – *in German*. No such German manuscript is preserved. But
there exists an English manuscript in Russell's hand entitled "Wittgenstein" and bearing the sub-headings "First MS", "2nd MS", "3rd
MS", and "4th MS". They evidently are Russell's translations into
English of a German manuscript (in four parts) which Wittgenstein
had sent to Russell after their meeting at Cambridge (see R.19). Since
he (R.19) refers to it as "copy", he must himself have copied (perhaps
excerpted) it from his originals. Later the same winter Russell made a
re-arrangement of the entire stuff, providing headings for its main sec-
tions. This re-arrangement is the so-called Costello version of the
"Notes on Logic", later published in the 1914–1916 *Notebooks*. There
is no indication that Wittgenstein had had a hand in *this* composition.

R.19   c/o H. Draegni, Skjolden
                                          Sogn, Norway
                                          29.10.13.

DEAR RUSSELL,

I hope you have got my letter which I wrote on the 16th. I left it in the Dining room of the boat and afterwards telephoned that it should be posted but I don't know with what effect. This is an ideal place to work in. – Soon after I arrived here I got a violent influenza which prevented me from doing any work until quite recently. Identity is the very Devil and *immensely important*; *very* much more so than I thought. It hangs – like everything else – directly together with the most fundamental questions, especially with the questions concerning the occurrence of the SAME argument in different places of a function. I have all sorts of ideas for a solution of the problem but could not yet arrive at anything definite. However I don't lose courage and go on thinking. – I have got two nice rooms here in the Postmaster's house and am looked after very well indeed. By the way – would you be so good and send me *two* copies of Moore's paper: "The Nature and Reality of Objects of Perception" which he read to the Aristotelian Soc[iety] in 1906. I am afraid I can't yet tell you the reason why I want *two* copies but you shall know it some day. If you kindly send the bill with them I will send the money immediately after receiving the Pamphlets. – As I hardly meet a soul in this place, the progress of my Norwegian is exceedingly slow; so much so that I have not yet learned a single swear-word. Please remember me to Dr and Mrs Whitehead and Erik if you see them. Write to me SOON.

                                  Yours as long as E! L.W.

P.S. How are your conversation-classes going on? Did you get the copy of my manuscript? I enclose a roseleaf as sample of the flora in this place.

                                                    30.10.

I wrote this letter yesterday. Since then quite new ideas have come into my head; new problems have arisen in the theory of molecular prop[osition]s and the theory of inference has received a new and very important aspect. One of the consequences of my new ideas will – I think – be that the whole of Logic follows from one P.p. only!! I cannot say more about it at present.

L.W.

Erik. – A son of the Whiteheads, subsequently killed in the Great War.

copy of my manuscript. – See comment to R.18.

R.20   [Skjolden, Sogn, Norway]
                                        [November 1913]

DEAR RUSSELL,

Thanks for your letter and the typed stuff! I will begin by
answering your questions as well as I can:

(1) Your question was – I think – due to the misprint (polarity
instead of *bi*polarity). What I mean to say is that we *only* then
understand a prop[osition] if we know *both* what would be the
case if it was *false and* what if it was *true*.

(2) The symbol for ~p is a—b—p—a—b. The prop[osition] *p*
has two poles and it does not matter a hang where they stand you
might just as well write ~p like this:

a—b
    ⟩ p   or   b—a—p—b—a   etc., etc.
b—a

all that *is* important is that the new *a*-pole should be correlated to
the old *b*-pole and vice versa WHEREVER THESE OLD POLES MAY
STAND. If you had only remembered the WF scheme of ~p you
would never have asked this question (I think). In fact all rules of
the ab symbolism follow directly from the essence of the WF
scheme.

(3) Whether ab-f[unctio]ns and your truth-f[unctio]ns are the
same cannot yet be decided.

(4) "The correlation of new poles is to be transitive" means
that by correlating one pole in the symbolizing way to another
and the other to a third we have *thereby* correlated the first in the
symbolizing way to the third, etc. For instance in

$$a\underset{\equiv}{—}b\underset{\equiv}{—}a\underset{=}{—}bpa\underset{\cdot}{—}b\underset{\equiv}{—}a\underset{\equiv}{—}b$$

a and b are correlated to $\underline{b}$ and $\underline{a}$ respectively and this means that
$\underset{\equiv}{}$ $\underset{\equiv}{}$
our symbol is the same as a—bpa—b.

(5) (p) p ∨ ~p *is* derived from *the function* p ∨ ~q but the point
will only become quite clear when identity is clear (as you said).
I will some other time write to you about this matter at length.

(6) Explanation in the typed stuff.

(7) You say, you thought that Bedeutung was the "fact", this is quite true, but remember that there are no such Things as facts and that therefore this prop[osition] itself wants analysing! If we speak of "die Bedeutung" we seem to be speaking of a Thing with a proper name. Of course the symbol for "a fact" is a prop-[osition] and this is *no* incomplete symbol.

(8) The exact ab-indefinable is given in the manuscript.

(9) An account of general indefinables? Oh Lord! It is *too* boring!!! Some other time! – Honestly – I *will* write to you about it some time, if by that time you have not found out all about it. (Because it is all quite clear in the manuscript, I think). But just now I am SO troubled with Identity that I really cannot write any long jaw. All sorts of new logical stuff seems to be growing in me, but I can't yet write about it.

Would you do me a great favour: I have promised last year to book *two* serial tickets for the C.U.M.S. Chamber Concerts. Would you kindly book them for me, keep one of them for yourself, give the other to somebody else and charge me for both. If you let me know the price I shall send you the money *at once*.

Pray for me and God bless you! (If there is such a thing).

Yours as long as

$$(\exists x).x = L.W.*$$

* This prop[osition] will probably turn out to have no meaning.

Write again soon.

the typed stuff. – See comment on R.18.
Bedeutung. – "Meaning", nowadays often translated "reference".
the manuscript. – See comment on R.18.
C.U.M.S. – Cambridge University Musical Society.

R.*21*   [Skjolden, Sogn, Norway]
                                          [November 1913]

DEAR RUSSELL,

There is the Cheque for 42 Kroner. Thanks very much for having bought the tickets. You haven't yet sent me Miss Harwood's
bill! – The following is a list of the questions you asked me in
your letter of the 25th.10.:

(1) "What is the point of 'p. ≡ . 'p' is true'? I mean why is it
worth saying[?]"

(2) "If 'apb' is the symbol for p, is 'bpa' the symbol for ∼p?
and if not, what is?["]

(3) "What you call ab-functions are what the Principia calls
'truth-f[unctio]ns'. I don't see why you shouldn't stick to the name
'truth-f[unctio]ns'."

(4) "I don't understand your rules about *a*'s and *b*'s, i.e. 'the
correlation of new poles is to be transitive'."

(5) (Is obvious from my letter.) So is (6).

(7) "You say 'Weder der Sinn noch die Bedeutung eines Satzes
ist ein Ding. Jene Worte sind unvollständige Zeichen'. I understand neither being a *thing*, but I thought the Bedeutung was the
fact, which is surely not indicated by an incomplete symbol?"

I don't know whether I have answered the question (7) clearly.
The answer is *of course* this: The Bedeutung of a prop[osition] is
symbolized by the proposition – which is *of course* not an incomplete symbol, *but the word "Bedeutung"* is an incomplete symbol.

(8) and (9) are obvious.

Write soon!

                                          Yours
                                          L.W.

Weder der Sinn . . . Zeichen. – "Neither the sense nor the meaning of a
proposition is a thing. These words are incomplete symbols."

R.*22*   [Skjolden, Sogn, Norway]
                                         [November 1913]

LIEBER RUSSELL,

I intended to write this letter in German, but it struck me that I did not know whether to call you "Sie" or "Du" and so I am reduced to my beastly English jargon! –

I will begin by explaining why there must be a prop[osition] from which all Logic follows:

I beg you to notice that, although I shall make use in what follows of my ab-Notation, the Meaning of this Notation is not needed; that is to say, even if this Notation should turn out not to be the final correct Notation what I am going to say is valid if you only admit – as I believe you must do – that it is a *possible* Notation. Now listen: I will first talk about those logical prop[osition]s which are or might be contained in the first 8 Chapters of Princ[ipia] Math[ematica]. That they all follow from *one* Pp is clear enough because ONE *symbolic rule* is sufficient to recognize each of them as true or false. And this is the *one* symbolic rule: write the prop[osition] down in the ab-Notation, trace all Connections (of Poles) from the outside to the inside Poles: Then if the b-Pole is connected to such *groups of inside Poles* ONLY *as contain opposite poles of* ONE *prop[osition]*, then the whole prop[osition] is a true, logical prop[osition]. If on the other hand this is the case with the a-Pole the prop[osition] is false and logical. If finally neither is the case the prop[osition] may be true or false but is in no case logical. Such for instance (p). $\sim$p – p limited to a suitable type of course – is not a logical prop[osition] at all and its truth can neither be proved nor disproved from logical pro[position]s alone. The same is the case – by the way – with your axiom of reducibility – *it is not a logical Prop[osition] at all* and the same applies to the axioms of infinity and the mult[iplicative] ax[iom]. IF *these are true prop[osition]s* they are *what I shall call "accidentally" true and not "essentially" true.* Whether a prop[osition] is accidentally or essentially true can be seen by writing it down in the ab-Notation and applying the above rule. What I – in stating this rule – called "logical" prop[osition] is a prop[osition] which is either essentially true or essentially false. This distinction of accid[entally] and essent[ially] true prop[osition]s explains – by the way – the feeling one always had about the infin[ity] ax[iom] and the axiom of reducibility, the feeling that if they were true they would be so only by a lucky accident.

Of course the rule I have given applies first of all only for what you called elementary prop[osition]s. But it is easy to see that it must also apply to all others. For consider your two Pps in the Theory of app[arent] var[iable]s *9.1 and *9.11. Put there instead of φx, $(\exists y) . \varphi y . y = x$ and it becomes obvious that the special cases of these two Pps like those of all the previous ones becomes tautologous if you apply the ab-Notation. The ab-Notation for Identity is not yet clear enough to show this clearly but it is obvious that such a Notation can be made up. I can sum up by saying that a logical prop[osition] is one the special cases of which are either tautologous – and then the prop[osition] is true – or "self-contradictory" (as I shall call it) and then it is false. And the ab-Notation simply shows directly which of those two it is (if any). That means that there is *one* Method of proving or disproving all logical prop[osition]s and this is: writing them down in the ab-Notation and looking at the connections and applying the above rule. But if *one* symbolic rule will do, there must also be *one* P.p. that will do. There is much that follows from all this and much that I could only explain vaguely but if you really think it over you will find that I am right. – I am glad that your classes are a success. As to Wiener I can only say that, if he is good at Math[ematics], Math[ematics] isn't much good. However –

Write again soon! And think always well of your

L.W.

P.S. Please remember me to Hardy. Every letter of yours gives me infinite pleasure!

Letter dated by Russell.

elementary propositions. – "A proposition which contains no apparent variables is called 'elementary'." *Principia Mathematica*, vol. I, p. 127.

your two Pps in the theory of app[arent] var[iable]s. – The two primitive propositions are:

*9.1   ⊢:φx.⊃.(∃z).φz   Pp
*9.11   ⊢:φx ∨ φy.⊃.(∃z)φz   Pp

Wiener. – The reference is evidently to Norbert Wiener, who had received his Ph.D. from Harvard in June 1913 and was now continuing his studies under Russell at Cambridge, England. Wittgenstein presumably met Wiener during his visit to Cambridge earlier in the autumn.

Hardy. – The mathematician G. H. Hardy (1877–1947).

In this and the next letter Wittgenstein explains the essentials of his decision procedure for the propositional calculus. The invention was evidently made roughly at the time at which Wittgenstein wrote this letter. The method is the one explained in *Tractatus* 6.1203. It is not the same as the now familiar truth-table method. The remark 6.1203, interestingly enough, does not occur in the *Prototractatus* manuscript or in the typescripts for the book. It was, we know, added only after the completion of the work when Wittgenstein was a prisoner of war at Cassino. (See *Prototractatus*, edited by B. F. McGuinness, T. Nyberg, and G. H. von Wright, with an historical introduction by G. H. von Wright. Routledge & Kegan Paul, London 1971, p. 11.) It is interesting that Wittgenstein should have been working on the problem of applying the ab-Notation to formulas involving identity with a view to inventing a decision procedure for them, too. He never solved the problem. It is also interesting that he was looking for a decision method for the whole realm of logical truth. This problem, as we now know, cannot be solved.

R.*23* [Skjolden, Sogn, Norway]
[November or December 1913]

LIEBER RUSSELL!

Vielen Dank für Deinen lieben Brief. Ich will dasjenige, was ich in meinem letzten Brief über Logik schrieb, noch einmal in anderer Weise wiederholen: Alle Sätze der Logik sind Verallgemeinerungen von Tautologien und alle Verallgemeinerungen von Tautologien sind Sätze der Logik. Andere logische Sätze gibt es nicht. (Dies halte ich für definitiv.) Ein Satz wie „$(\exists x).x=x$" z.B. ist eigentlich ein Satz der *Physik*. Der Satz

$$„(x):x=x.\supset.(\exists y).y=y"$$

ist ein Satz der Logik; es ist nun Sache der *Physik* zu sagen, *ob es ein Ding gibt*. Dasselbe gilt vom infin[ity] ax[iom]; ob es $\aleph_0$ Dinge gibt, das zu bestimmen ist Sache der Erfahrung (und die kann es nicht entscheiden). Nun aber zu Deinem Reductions-Axiom: Stell' Dir vor, wir lebten in einer Welt, worin es nichts als $\aleph_0$ *Dinge* gäbe und außerdem NUR *noch eine* Relation, welche zwischen unendlich vielen dieser Dinge bestehe und zwar so, daß sie nicht zwischen jedem Ding und jedem anderen besteht, und daß sie ferners auch nie zwischen einer endlichen Anzahl von Dingen besteht. Es ist klar, daß das ax[iom] of Red[ucibility] in einer solchen Welt sicher *nicht* bestünde. Es ist mir aber auch klar, daß es nicht die Sache der Logik ist darüber zu entscheiden, ob die Welt worin wir leben nun wirklich so ist, oder nicht. Was aber Tautologien eigentlich sind, das kann ich selber noch nicht ganz klar sagen, will aber trachten es ungefähr zu erklären. Es ist das eigentümliche (und *höchst* wichtige) Merkmal der *nicht*-logischen Sätze, daß man ihre Wahrheit *nicht* am Satzzeichen selbst erkennen kann. Wenn ich z.B. sage „Meier ist dumm", so kannst Du dadurch, daß Du diesen Satz anschaust, nicht sagen ob er wahr oder falsch ist. Die Sätze der Logik aber – und sie allein – haben die Eigenschaft, daß sich ihre Wahrheit bezw. Falschheit schon in ihrem Zeichen ausdrückt. Es ist mir noch nicht gelungen, für die Identität eine Bezeichnung zu finden, die dieser Bedingung genügt; aber *ich zweifle* NICHT, daß sich eine solche Bezeichnungsweise finden lassen muß. Für zusammengesetzte Sätze (elem[entary] prop[ositions]) genügt die ab-Bezeichnungsw[eise]. Es ist mir unangenehm, daß Du die Zeichenregel aus meinem letzten Brief nicht verstanden hast, denn es langweilt mich UNSAGBAR sie zu erklären!! Du könntest sie auch durch ein bißchen Nach denken selber finden!

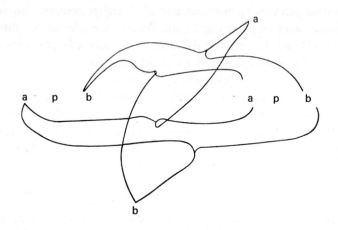

Dies ist das Zeichen für⁻p ≡ p; es ist tautologisch weil *b* nur mit solchen Pol-paaren verbunden ist, welche aus den entgegenge-setzten Polen eines Satzes (nämlich p) bestehen; wenn Du dies auf Sätze anwendest, die mehr als 2 Argumente haben so erhältst Du die allgemeine Regel, wonach Tautologien gebildet werden. Ich bitte Dich denke selbst über die Sachen nach, es ist mir SCHRECKLICH eine schriftliche Erklärung zu wiederholen, die ich schon zum ersten Mal mit dem aller *größten Widerstreben* gege-ben habe. Die Identität ist mir – wie gesagt – noch gar nicht klar. Also hierüber ein andermal! Wenn Dein Ax[iom] of Red[uci-bility] fällt, so wird wahrscheinlich manches geändert werden müßen. Warum gebrauchst Du als Definition der Klassen nicht diese:

$$F[\hat{x}(\varphi x)]. = :\varphi z \equiv_z \psi z. \supset_\psi . F(\psi) \quad \text{Def?}$$

– Zu Weihnachten werde ich LEIDER nach Wien fahren müssen.

Meine Mutter nämlich wünscht es sich so sehr, daß sie schwer gekränkt wäre, wenn ich nicht käme; und sie hat vom vorigen Jahr gerade an diese Zeit so böse Erinnerungen, daß ich es nicht über's Herz bringen kann wegzubleiben. Ich werde aber sehr bald wieder hierher zurückkehren. Meine Stimmung ist mittelmäßig, weil meine Arbeit nicht rasch vorwärts geht und weil mir der Gedanke an meine Heimfahrt entsetzlich ist. Die Einsamkeit hier tut mir unendlich wohl und ich glaube, daß ich das Leben unter Menschen jetzt nicht vertrüge. In mir gärt alles! Die große Frage ist jetzt: Wie muß ein Zeichensystem beschaffen sein, damit es jede Tautologie AUF EINE UND DIESELBE WEISE als Tautologie erkennen läßt? Dies ist das Grundproblem der Logik! – Ich bin überzeugt, ich werde in meinem Leben nie etwas veröffentlichen. Aber nach meinem Tod mußt Du den Band meines Tagebuchs, worin die ganze Geschichte steht, drucken lassen. *Schreib bald hierher* und versuche aus meinen verwirrten Erklärungen klar zu werden.

Immer Dein

L.W.

P.S. Deine Briefe sind mir eine große Wohltat; laß es Dich nicht reuen, mir so oft zu schreiben. Ich will nur noch sagen, daß Deine Theorie der „Descriptions" *ganz* ZWEIFELLOS richtig ist, selbst wenn die einzelnen Urzeichen darin ganz andere sind als Du glaubtest.

– Ich glaube oft daß ich verrückt werde.

(R.*23 English Translation*)

DEAR RUSSELL,

Many thanks for your kind letter. I want to repeat again, in a different form, what I wrote about logic in my last letter. All the propositions of logic are generalizations of tautologies and all generalizations of tautologies are propositions of logic. There are no other logical propositions. (I regard this as definitive.) A proposition such as "$(\exists x).x=x$", for example, is really a proposition of *physics*. The proposition

$$"(x):x=x.\supset.(\exists y).y=y"$$

is a proposition of logic and it is then for *physics* to say *whether any thing exists*. The same holds for the axiom of infinity: whether there exist $\aleph_0$ things is a matter for experience to determine (and one which experience cannot decide). But now, as to your Axiom of Reduction: imagine we lived in a world in which nothing existed except $\aleph_0$ *things* and, over and above them, ONLY a *single* relation holding between infinitely many of the things and in such a way that it did not hold between each thing and every other thing and further never held between a finite number of things. It is clear that the axiom of reducibility would certainly *not* hold good in such a world. But it is also clear to me that whether or not the world in which we live is really of this kind is not a matter for logic to decide. As to what tautologies really are, however, I my-self am not yet able to say quite clearly but I will try to give a rough explanation. It is the peculiar (and *most* important) mark of *non*-logical propositions that one is *not* able to recognize their truth from the propositional sign alone. If I say, for example, "Meier is stupid", you cannot tell by looking at this proposition whether it is true or false. But the propositions of logic – and only they – have the property that their truth or falsity, as the case may be, finds its expression in the very sign for the proposition. I have not yet succeeded in finding a notation for identity that satisfies this condition; but *I have* NO *doubt* that it must be possible to find such a notation. For compound propositions ("elementary pro-positions") the ab-notation is sufficient. It distresses me that you did not understand the rule dealing with signs in my last letter because it bores me BEYOND WORDS to explain it. If you thought about it for a bit you could discover it for yourself!

This* is the sign for $p\equiv p$: it is tautological because *b* is con-nected only with those pairs of poles that consist of opposite poles of a single proposition (namely p). Apply this to proposi-tions with more than two arguments and you will obtain the general rule for the construction of tautologies. I beg you to think about these matters for yourself: it is INTOLERABLE for me, to repeat a written explanation which even the first time I gave only with the *utmost repugnance*. I find identity, as I say, still far from clear. So I will deal with that another time. If your axiom of re-ducibility fails, then probably a lot of things will have to be

*Here given opposite.

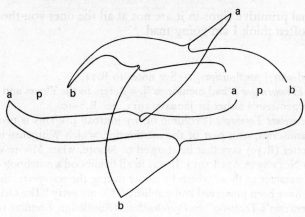

changed. Why do not you use the following as the definition of a class

$$F[\hat{x}(\varphi x)] . = : \varphi z \equiv_z \psi z . \supset_\psi . F(\psi) \quad \text{Def?}$$

– At Christmas I must UNFORTUNATELY go to Vienna.

The fact is, my mother very much wants me to, so much so that she would be grievously offended if I did not come; and she has such bad memories of just this time last year that I have not the heart to stay away. But I shall return here very early. I am in mediocre spirits because my work is not progressing rapidly and because the thought of going back home appals me. Being alone here does me no end of good and I do not think I could now bear life among people. Inside me, everything is in a state of ferment. The big question now is, how must a system of signs be constituted in order to make every tautology recognizable as such IN ONE AND THE SAME WAY? This is the fundamental problem of logic! – I am convinced I shall never publish anything in my lifetime. But after my death you must see to the printing of the volume of my journal with the whole story in it. *Write here soon* and try to understand my muddled explanations.

Yours ever,
L.W.

P.S. Your letters are a great boon to me. Do not feel sorry for writing to me so often. I only want to add that your "Theory of Descriptions" is *quite* CERTAINLY correct, even though the in-

dividual primitive signs in it are not at all the ones you thought.
– I often think I am going mad.

(*elem*[*entary*] *prop*[*ositions*]). – See notes to R.22.

böse Erinnerungen ["bad memories"]. – Refers to the illness and death
of Wittgenstein's father in January 1913. See R.7–10.

Band meines Tagebuchs ["volume of my journal"]. – This is probably
the manuscript, or a part of the manuscript, which Wittgenstein in a
later letter (R.30) says that he showed to Moore, when Moore visited
him in Norway in April 1914. It was in all likelihood a notebook of the
same character as those which he wrote during the war-years, three of
which have been preserved and published. Cf. my essay "The Origin of
Wittgenstein's *Tractatus*" in *Prototractatus* (Routledge, London 1971).

R.*24*   Skjolden, Sogn
                                          15.12.13.

LIEBER RUSSELL!

Ich schicke heute 720 Kroner an Messrs Child & Co. für Deine
Rechnung. Die Frage nach dem Wesen der Identität läßt sich
nicht beantworten, ehe das Wesen der Tautologie erklärt ist. Die
Frage nach diesem aber, ist die Grundfrage *aller* Logik. – Mein
Tag vergeht zwischen Logik, Pfeifen, Spazierengehen und Nie-
dergeschlagensein. Ich wollte zu Gott, ich hätte mehr Verstand
und es würde mir nun endlich alles klar; oder ich müßte nicht
mehr lange leben! –

Du hast die Eroika gehört! Was hast Du zu dem zweiten Satz
gesagt? ist er nicht unglaublich? –

Ist es nicht höchst merkwürdig, was für eine große und unendlich eigenartige Wissenschaft die Logik ist; ich glaube, weder Du
noch ich haben das vor 1½ Jahren gewußt.

                                          Immer Dein
                                          L.W.

(R.*24 English Translation*)

DEAR RUSSELL,

I am sending Messrs Child & Co. 720 Kroner today for credit
to your account. The question as to the nature of identity cannot
be answered until the nature of tautology has been explained. But
that question is fundamental to the *whole* of logic. – My day passes
between logic, whistling, going for walks, and being depressed. I
wish to God that I were more intelligent and everything would
finally become clear to me – or else that I needn't live much
longer! –

You heard the Eroica! What did you think of the second move-
ment? Isn't it incredible? –

It's extraordinary, isn't it, what a huge and infinitely strange
science logic is? Neither you nor I knew that, I think, a year and a
half ago.

                                          Yours ever
                                          L.W.

R.*25*   Skjolden
                                          [January 1914]

Lieber Russell!

Vielen Dank für Deinen lieben Brief! leider kann ich Dir auch
diesmal wieder keine logischen Neuigkeiten berichten: denn es
ist mir in den letzten Wochen fürchterlich schlecht gegangen.
(Eine Folge meiner Wiener „Ferien".) Ich war jeden Tag abwech-
selnd von schrecklicher Angst und Depression gequält und selbst
wenn diese aussetzten so erschöpft, daß ich an ein Arbeiten gar
nicht denken konnte. Die Möglichkeiten der geistigen Qual sind
unsagbar entsetzlich! Erst seit zwei Tagen kann ich wieder die
Stimme der Vernunft durch den Lärm der Gespenster hören und
habe wieder angefangen zu arbeiten. Und *vielleicht* werde ich jetzt
genesen und etwas anständiges hervorbringen können. Aber ich
habe *nie* gewußt, was es heißt, sich nur noch *einen* Schritt vom
Wahnsinn zu fühlen. – Hoffen wir das Beste! –

Ja, Mörike ist freilich ein *großer* Dichter und seine Gedichte ge-
hören zum besten was wir haben. Aber ich bin neugierig, ob Du
ihn wirklich genießen wirst, weil Du doch Goethe nicht genießest.
Und Mörikes Schönheit ist ganz nahe verwandt mit Goethes.
Aber *wenn* Du Mörike *wirklich* genoßen hast, dann versuch' einmal die Iphigenie von Goethe: vielleicht geht Dir dann ein Licht
auf. –

Jetzt noch eine Frage: Sagt der „Satz vom zureichenden
Grunde" (Law of causality) nicht einfach, daß Raum und Zeit relativ sind? Dies scheint mir jetzt ganz klar zu sein; denn alle die
Ereignisse von denen dieser Satz behaupten soll, daß sie nicht eintreten können, könnten überhaupt nur in einer absoluten Zeit und
einem absoluten Raum eintreten. (Dies wäre freilich noch kein
unbedingter Grund zu meiner Behauptung.) Aber denke an den
Fall des Massenteilchens, das, allein in der Welt existierend, und
seit aller Ewigkeit in Ruhe, plötzlich im Zeitpunkt A anfängt sich
zu bewegen; und denke an ähnliche Fälle, so wirst Du – glaube
ich sehen – daß keine Einsicht a priori uns solche Ereignisse als
unmöglich erscheinen läßt, *außer eben in dem Fall* daß Raum und

Zeit relativ sind. Bitte schreibe mir Deine Meinung in diesem Punkte.

Ich wünsche Dir alles Beste zu Deinen Vorlesungen in Amerika. Vielleicht geben sie Dir doch Gelegenheit mehr als sonst Deine *Gedanken* und nicht *nur* fertig formulierte Resultate auszusprechen. Und DAS gerade wäre von dem denkbar größten Wert für Deine Hörer, wenn sie den Wert des *Gedankens,* nicht den des fertigen Resultats, kennen lernten. Schreib' mir bald und denk' an mich, wenn Du im Mörike liesest.

Immer Dein

L.W.

P.S. Noch eine Bitte! Ich schicke Dir beiligend meine College-Rechnung und einen Check für 80 Kroner; ich bitte Dich hiervon die Rechnung zu zahlen, da ich nicht weiß, ob Barclay & Co. Norwegisches Geld annimmt.

I[mmer] D[ein]

L.W.

(R.25 English Translation)

DEAR RUSSELL,

Many thanks for your kind letter. It's VERY sad but I've once again no logical news for you. The reason is that things have gone terribly badly for me in the last weeks. (A result of my "holidays" in Vienna.) Every day I was tormented by a frightful *Angst* and by depression in turns and even in the intervals I was so exhausted that I wasn't able to think of doing a bit of work. It's terrifying beyond all description the kinds of mental torment that there can be! It wasn't until two days ago that I could hear the voice of reason over the howls of the damned and I began to work again. And *perhaps* I'll get better now and be able to produce something decent. But I *never* knew what it meant to feel only *one* step away from madness. – Let's hope for the best! –

Yes: Mörike really is a *great* poet and his poems are part of the best of what we have. But I am curious to know whether you will really enjoy him. After all, you don't enjoy Goethe and the beauty of Mörike's work is very closely related to that of Goethe's. But *if* you have *really* enjoyed Mörike, then just try Goethe's *Iphigenie*. Then perhaps you'll see the light.

Now for a question: isn't what the "principle of sufficient reason" (law of causality) says simply that space and time are relative? I now think this is quite obvious, because all the events which, according to this assertion, are not meant to be possible could only occur, if at all, in an absolute time and space. (Admittedly this wouldn't in itself be an adequate reason for my assertion.) But think of the case of a particle that is the only thing existing in the world and that has been at rest for all eternity and that suddenly, at time *A*, begins to move. Think of this and similar cases and you will see, I believe, that it is NOT an a priori insight that makes such events seem impossible to us *unless it is the case* that space and time are relative. Please write and tell me your opinion on this point.

All best wishes for your lecture-course in America! Perhaps it will give you at any rate a more favourable opportunity than usual to tell them your *thoughts* and not *just* cut and dried results. THAT is what would be of the greatest imaginable value for your audience – to get to know the value of *thought* and not that of a cut and dried result. Write to me soon and think of me when you read Mörike.

Yours ever

L.W.

P.S. Another request! I enclose my College bill and a cheque for 80 Kroner. Please pay the bill out of this, because I don't know whether Barclay & Co. will accept Norwegian money.

Yours ever

L.W.

Vorlesungen in Amerika ["lecture-course in America"]. – Refers perhaps to the Lowell Lectures which Russell gave at the Lowell Institute in Boston in March and April 1914 and subsequently published under the title *Our Knowledge of the External World;* or to either or both of the courses, on Theory of Knowledge and Advanced Logic, given in the Department of Philosophy, Harvard University, during the same period.

R.*26*   [Skjolden, Sogn, Norway]
                               [January or February 1914]
LIEBER RUSSELL!

Ich danke Dir für Deinen freundlichen Brief. Es war sehr
schön von Dir, daß Du mir auf diese Weise geantwortet hast!
Deine Forderung aber, ich solle so tun als sei nichts vorgefallen,
kann ich Dir unmöglich erfüllen, da dies ganz gegen meine Natur
ginge. VERZEIH *mir daher diesen langen Brief* und bedenke daß ich
meiner Natur ebenso folgen *muß*, wie Du der Deinen. Ich habe in
der letzten Woche viel über unser Verhältnis nachgedacht und
bin zu dem Schluß gekommen, daß wir eigentlich nicht zu einander passen. DIES MEINE ICH NICHT ALS TADEL! weder für Dich
noch für mich. Aber es ist eine Tatsache. Wir hatten ja schon so
oft ungemütliche Gespräche mit einander, wenn wir auf gewisse
Themen kamen. Und die Ungemütlichkeit war nicht eine Folge
von schlechter Laune auf seiten eines von uns beiden, sondern sie
war die Folge enormer Unterschiede in unserem Wesen. Ich bitte
Dich inständigst nicht zu glauben, ich wolle Dich irgendwie ta-
deln, oder Dir eine Predigt halten; sondern ich will nur unser Verhältnis klarlegen *weil ich daraus einen Schluß ziehen werde.* – Auch
unser letzter Streit war bestimmt nicht bloß die Folge Deiner
Empfindlichkeit oder meiner Rücksichtslosigkeit, sondern der
tiefere Grund lag darin, daß Dir jener Brief von mir zeigen
mußte, wie grundverschieden unsere Auffassungen z.B. des
Wertes eines wissenschaftlichen Werkes sind. Es war natürlich
dumm von mir, Dir damals so lang über jene Sache geschrieben
zu haben, denn ich hätte mir ja sagen müßen, daß sich solche
wesentliche Unterschiede nicht durch einen Brief ausgleichen
lassen. Und dies ist ja nur EIN Fall unter *vielen.* Ich sehe jetzt, wo
ich dies in aller Ruhe schreibe, vollkommen ein, daß Deine Werturteile ebenso gut sind und ebenso tief in Dir begründet sind wie
meine in mir, und daß ich kein Recht habe Dich zu katechisieren;
aber ebenso klar sehe ich jetzt, daß wir eben darum kein rechtes
Freundschaftsverhältnis zu einander haben können. *Ich werde Dir*
so lange ich lebe vom GANZEM HERZEN *dankbar und zugetan sein, aber*
ich werde Dir nicht mehr schreiben und Du wirst mich auch nicht mehr

sehen. Jetzt wo ich mich mit Dir wieder versöhnt habe, will ich *in Frieden* von Dir scheiden, damit wir nicht irgend einmal wieder gegen einander gereizt werden und dann vielleicht in Feindschaft auseinander gehen. Ich wünsche Dir alles Beste und bitte Dich mich nicht zu vergessen und oft *freundlich* an mich zu denken. Leb wohl!

Immer Dein

LUDWIG WITTGENSTEIN

(R.*26 English Translation*)

DEAR RUSSELL,

Thank you for your friendly letter. It was very good of you to answer me in such a way. But I can't possibly carry out your request to behave as if nothing had happened: that would go clean contrary to my nature. *So* FORGIVE *me for this long letter* and remember that I *have to* follow my nature just as much as you. During the last week I have thought a lot about our relationship and I have come to the conclusion that we really don't suit one another. THIS IS NOT MEANT AS A REPROACH! either for you or for me. But it is a fact. We've often had uncomfortable conversations with one another when certain subjects came up. And the uncomfortableness was not a consequence of ill humour on one side or the other but of enormous differences in our natures. I beg you most earnestly not to think I want to reproach you in any way or to preach you a sermon. I only want to put our relationship in clear terms *in order to draw a conclusion.* – Our latest quarrel, too, was certainly not simply a result of your sensitiveness or my inconsiderateness. It came from deeper – from the fact that my letter must have shown you how totally different our ideas are, E.G. of the value of a scientific work. It was, of course, stupid of me to have written to you at such length about this matter: I ought to have told myself that such fundamental differences cannot be resolved by a letter. And this is just ONE instance out of *many*. Now, as I'm writing this in complete calm, I can see perfectly well that your value-judgments are just as good and just as deep-seated in you as mine in me, and that I have no right to catechize you. But I see equally clearly, now, that for that very reason there cannot be any real relation of friendship between us. *I shall be grateful to you and devoted to you* WITH ALL MY HEART *for the whole of my life, but I shall not write to you again and you will not see me again either.* Now that I am once again reconciled with you I want to part from you *in peace* so that we shan't sometime get annoyed with one another again and then perhaps part as enemies. I wish you everything of the best and I beg you not to forget me and to think of me often *with friendly feelings.* Goodbye!

Yours *ever*

LUDWIG WITTGENSTEIN

In this and the next letter there is reference to a quarrel (*Streit*) between Wittgenstein and Russell. About it nothing more is known than what the two letters tell us. In all probability there must have existed at least one letter from Wittgenstein to Russell which Russell destroyed.

R.27   Skjolden
                                               3.3.14.

LIEBER RUSSELL!

Dein Brief war *so* voll von Güte und Freundschaft, daß ich nicht glaube, auf ihn schweigen zu *dürfen*. Ich muß also mein Vorhaben brechen: was ich Dir aber sagen muß, kann ich leider nicht kurz fassen und ich habe kaum irgendwelche Hoffnung, daß Du mich wirklich verstehen wirst. Vor allem muß ich nocheinmal sagen: Unsere Streitigkeiten kommen nicht *nur* aus äußerlichen Gründen (Nervosität, Übermüdung u. dgl.) sondern sind – jedenfalls in *mir – sehr* tief begründet. Du magst darin recht haben, daß *wir selbst* vielleicht nicht einmal *so sehr* verschieden sind: aber *unsere Ideale* sind es ganz und gar. Und darum konnten und können wir *nie* über Dinge, worin unsere Werturteile in Betracht kamen, mit einander reden, ohne zu heucheln, oder zu zanken. *Ich glaube dies läßt sich nicht leugnen* und war mir schon seit langer Zeit aufgefallen; und war mir schrecklich, denn unser Verkehr bekam dadurch etwas vom Beisammensitzen in einem Sumpfe. Denn wir beide haben Schwächen, besonders aber *ich* und mein Leben ist VOLL von den häßlichsten und kleinlichsten Gedanken und Taten (dies ist *keine* Übertreibung). Wenn aber ein Verkehr nicht beide Teile herabziehen soll, dann dürfen die *Schwächen* der beiden *nicht* mit einander verkehren. Sondern zwei Leute sollen nur dort mit einander verkehren, wo sie beide *rein* sind; d.i. dort wo sie gegen einander *ganz* offen sein können, ohne einander zu verletzen. Und *das* können wir beide NUR, wenn wir unseren Verkehr auf die Mitteilung objectiv feststellbarer Tatsachen beschränken und etwa noch auf die Mitteilung unserer freundschaftlichen Gefühle. Alle anderen Themen aber führen bei uns zur Heuchelei oder zum Zank. Du sagst vielleicht: es ist ja bisher so ziemlich gegangen, warum sollte es nicht so weitergehen. Aber ich bin des ewigen schmutzigen und halben ZU müde! Mein Leben war bisher *eine* große Schweinerei – aber soll es immer so weitergehen? – Ich schlage Dir nun dies vor: Machen wir einander Mitteilungen über unsere Arbeiten, unser Befinden und dergleichen, aber unterlassen wir gegen einander jedwedes Werturteil – worüber immer –, in dem vollen Bewußtsein, daß wir hierin gegen einander nicht *ganz* ehrlich sein könnten, ohne den anderen zu verletzen (zum mindesten gilt dies bestimmt von *mir*). Meiner tiefen Zuneigung brauche ich Dich nicht erst zu versichern, *aber sie wäre in großer Gefahr, wenn wir mit einem Verkehr fortführen, der Heuchelei zur Grundlage hat und deshalb für uns beide beschämend ist.* Aber ich glaube, es wäre ehrenvoll für uns beide, wenn wir ihn auf einer reineren Grundlage fortsetzten. – Ich bitte Dich, Dir dies alles zu überlegen, mir aber *nur dann* zu antworten, wenn Du es im Guten tun kannst. In jedem Fall sei meiner Liebe und Treue versichert. Möchtest Du diesen Brief so verstehen wie er gemeint ist!

Immer Dein
L.W.

(R.*27 English Translation*)

DEAR RUSSELL,

Your letter was *so* full of kindness and friendship that I don't think I have the *right* to leave it unanswered. So I have to break my resolution. Unfortunately, however, I can't put what I have to say to you in a few words and I have scarcely any hope that you'll really understand me. The chief thing, I must tell you again, is that our quarrels don't arise *just* from external reasons such as nervousness or over-tiredness but are – at any rate on *my* side – *very* deep-rooted. You may be right in saying that *we ourselves* are not *so very* different, but *our ideals* could not be more so. And that's why we haven't been able and we shan't *ever* be able to talk about anything involving our value-judgements without either becoming hypocritical or falling out. *I think this is incontestable*; I had noticed it a long time ago; and it was frightful for me, because it tainted our relations with one another: we seemed to be sitting side by side in a marsh. The fact is, we both of us have weaknesses, but especially *I* have, and my life is <u>FULL</u> of the ugliest and pettiest thoughts imaginable (this is *not* an exaggeration). But if a relationship is not to be degrading for both sides then it should *not* be a relationship between the weaknesses on either side. No: a relationship should be confined to areas where both

people involved have clean hands, i.e. where each can be completely frank without hurting the other. And that's something *we*
can do ONLY by restricting our relationship to the communication
of facts capable of being established objectively, with perhaps
also some mention of our friendly feelings for one another. But
any other subject will lead, in our case, to hypocrisy or to falling
out. Now perhaps, you'll say, "Things have more or less worked,
up to the present. Why not go on in the same way?" But I'm *too*
tired of this constant sordid compromise. My life has been one
nasty mess so far – but need that go on indefinitely? – Now, I'll
make a proposal to you. Let's write to each other about our work,
our health, and the like, but let's avoid in our communications any
kind of value-judgment, on any subject whatsoever, and let's recognize clearly that in such judgements neither of us could be
completely honest without hurting the other (this is certainly true
in *my* case, at any rate). I don't need to assure you of my deep
affection for you, *but that affection would be in great danger if we were
to continue with a relationship based on hypocrisy and for that reason a
source of shame to us both*. No, I think the honourable thing for both
of us would be if we continued it on a more genuine basis. – I beg
you to think this over and to send me an answer *only when* you can
do it without bitterness. Feel assured in any case of my love and
loyalty. I only hope you may understand this letter as it is meant
to be understood.

Yours ever

L.W.

R.*28*   [Skjolden, Sogn, Norway]

[Late April, May or June 1914]

LIEBER RUSSELL!

Nur ein paar Zeilen um Dir zu sagen daß ich Deinen l[ieben] Brief erhalten habe und daß meine Arbeit in den letzten 4–5 Monaten große Fortschritte gemacht hat. Jetzt aber bin ich wieder in einem Zustand der Ermüdung und kann weder arbeiten noch meine Arbeit erklären. Ich habe sie aber Moore als er bei mir war *ausführlich* erklärt und er hat sich verschiedenes aufgeschrieben. Du wirst also alles am besten von ihm erfahren können. Es ist viel Neues. – Am besten wirst Du alles verstehen wenn Du Moores Aufzeichnungen selber liesest. Es wird jetzt wohl wieder einige Zeit dauern bis ich wieder etwas hervorbringe. Bis dahin,

Dein

L.W.

P.S. Ich baue mir jetzt hier ein kleines Haus in der Einsamkeit. Hoffentlich war Deine Reise erfolgreich.

(R.*28 English Translation*)

DEAR RUSSELL,

Just a few lines to tell you that I received your kind letter and that my work has made considerable progress in the last four or five months. But I have now relapsed into a state of exhaustion and can neither do any work nor explain what I did earlier. However I explained it *in detail* to Moore when he was with me and he made various notes. So you can best find it all out from him. Many things in it are new. – The best way to understand it all would be if you read Moore's notes for yourself. It will probably be some time now before I produce anything further. Till then –

Yours

L.W.

P.S. I am now building myself a small house here miles from anyone. I hope your journey was a success.

Russell arrived back from the United States on June 14th. Wittgenstein may have known from Russell's letters to him, when Russell was supposed to return to England. If this is so, then the use of the past tense in "Hoffentlich war Deine Reise erfolgreich" would indicate that the letter was written in the middle or second half of June.

Moore's visit was from 29 March to 14 April. Wittgenstein seems to have returned to Austria from Norway about the turn of the months June–July. We know from M.9 that he was in Vienna in the beginning of July. Later in July he was at Hochreit and on the eve of the outbreak of the war again in Vienna. (See Ludwig Wittgenstein, *Briefe an Ludwig von Ficker*, Otto Müller Verlag, Salzburg 1969.)

Wittgenstein did not live in the hut he was building, before the war. After the war, in 1921, he visited the place in the company of his friend Arvid Sjögren and that was the first time he lived in the hut. He lived there again for the greater part of the academic year 1936–1937. (See M.28–30 and M.33.) It was then that he started work on the *Investigations*. His last visit to Skjolden was towards the end of 1950 in the company of his friend, Dr Ben Richards.

R.*29*   IV. Alleegasse 16
                                                [June or July 1914]

LIEBER RUSSELL!

Vielen Dank für Deinen Brief! Ich bin wie Du siehst zu Hause,
und LEIDER wieder einmal ganz unfruchtbar. Ich hoffe nur die
Ideen werden wiederkommen, wenn ich in meine Einsamkeit
zurückkehre. (Ich bleibe noch etwa 8–10 Tage hier.) Was Deine
amerikanischen Vorlesungen anbelangt, so brauchtest Du mich –
von *mir* aus – natürlich gar nicht zu nennen; aber – wie Du
willst –. Hier geht es mir jeden Tag anders: Einmal glaube ich,
ich werde verrückt, so stark gärt alles in mir; den nächsten Tag
bin ich wieder ganz und gar phlegmatisch. Am Grunde meiner
Seele aber kocht es fort und fort wie am Grunde eines Geisirs.
Und ich hoffe immer noch es werde endlich einmal ein endgültiger
Ausbruch erfolgen, und ich kann ein anderer Mensch werden.
Über Logik kann ich Dir heute nichts schreiben. Vielleicht
glaubst Du daß es Zeitverschwendung ist über mich selbst zu
denken; aber wie kann ich Logiker sein, wenn ich noch nicht
Mensch bin! *Vor allem* muß ich mit mir selbst in's Reine kommen!

                                                Immer Dein
                                                L.W.

(R.*29 English Translation*)

DEAR RUSSELL,

Many thanks for your letter. As you see, I am at home and UN-
FORTUNATELY once again quite unproductive. I only hope the
ideas will start to flow again when I go back into isolation. (I am
staying here for about another eight or ten days.) As regards your
American lecture-course, there was naturally no need at all, as far
as *I*'m concerned, to mention my name. But – as you wish –.
Here I feel different every day. Sometimes things inside me are in
such a ferment that I think I'm going mad: then the next day I am
totally apathetic again. But deep inside me there's a perpetual
seething, like the bottom of a geyser, and I keep on hoping that
things will come to an eruption once and for all, so that I can turn

into a different person. I can't write you anything about logic to-day. Perhaps you regard this thinking about myself as a waste of time – but how can I be a logician before I'm a human being! *Far* the most important thing is to settle accounts with myself!

Yours ever

L.W.

Russell dated this letter "Spring 1914". It is not known, however, that Wittgenstein was in Austria between the time of the Christmas holidays and his return in June–July. Also the use of the past tense in "brauchtest" would indicate that Wittgenstein is referring to something Russell had written in a letter *after* March and April, when he gave the Lowell Lectures, and during the time when he was preparing the book for publication. (There is a mention of Wittgenstein in the Preface, dated Cambridge June 1914, and in a footnote in the text.)

It is interesting that Wittgenstein states that he was going to remain in Vienna for only eight or ten days and then return to his isolation ("Einsamkeit"). It seems that he was thinking of going back to Nor-way. In a letter to his friend W. Eccles in Manchester, dated July 1914, Wittgenstein talks of going "for a journey in the middle of August" and of coming to England in September. (Cf. comments on R.28 above.)

R.*30*   [Received by Russell in January 1915]

LIEBER RUSSELL!

Erst heute erhielt ich Deinen lieben Brief, den Du am 28. Juli an mich geschrieben hast. Daß Moore meine Ideen Dir nicht hat erklären können, ist mir unbegreiflich. Hast Du aus seinen Notizen irgend etwas entnehmen können?? Ich fürchte, Nein! Sollte ich in diesem Krieg umkommen, so wird Dir mein Manuskript, welches ich damals Moore zeigte, zugeschickt werden; nebst einem, welches ich jetzt während des Krieges geschrieben habe. Im Falle ich am Leben bleibe, so möchte ich nach dem Kriege nach England kommen und Dir meine Arbeit – wenn es Dir recht ist – mündlich erklären. Ich bin auch im ersten Fall davon überzeugt, daß sie früher oder später von jemandem verstanden werden wird! Besten Dank für die Zusendung Deiner Schrift über Sense-Data. Ich habe sie noch nicht gelesen. Möge der Himmel mir bald wieder gute Ideen schenken!!! –

Dein

LUDWIG WITTGENSTEIN

Bitte grüße Johnson herzlichst!

Meine Adresse ist: Art[illerie] Autodetachement

„Oblt Gürth"

Feldpost No 186

(R.*30 English Translation*)

DEAR RUSSELL,

It was only today that I got your kind letter which you wrote me on 28th July. I find it inconceivable that Moore wasn't able to explain my ideas to you. Were you able to get anything at all out of his notes? I'm afraid the answer is, No. If I should not survive the present war, the manuscript of mine that I showed to Moore at the time will be sent to you, along with another one which I have written now, during the war. In the case that I am still alive, I should like to come to England after the war and explain my work to you orally, if you've no objection. Even in the former case, I'm convinced that it will be understood by somebody sooner or later. Thank you very much for sending your piece about sense-data. I haven't read it yet. Heaven send I'll have some good ideas again soon!!!

Yours

LUDWIG WITTGENSTEIN

Please remember me very kindly to Johnson.

My address is: Artillerie Autodetachement
      "Oblt Gürth"
      Feldpost No 186.

Notizen. – Refers to the Notes dictated by Wittgenstein to Moore in Norway, published as an appendix to *Notebooks 1914–1916.*

Manuskript. – The manuscript which Wittgenstein had shown to Moore in Norway is apparently lost; the manuscript written during the war must be the first of the posthumously published 1914–1916 notebooks.

Schrift über Sense-Data. – This must be "The Relation of Sense-Data to Physics", *Scientia 16*, July 1914 (reprinted in *Mysticism and Logic*).

Oblt. – Oberleutnant.

For Wittgenstein's military career during the first world war see the Editor's Appendix to Paul Engelmann, *Letters from Ludwig Wittgenstein, with a Memoir,* ed. by B. F. McGuinness, Basil Blackwell, Oxford 1967, pp. 140–142.

Russell's reply to this letter has been preserved and is the only letter from Russell to Wittgenstein which is known still to exist. (Cf. above, Introduction, p. 3.) The letter was given by Wittgenstein to a friend at Cambridge in the 1930's and is now in the Bertrand Russell Archives at McMaster University. It is here reprinted with the kind permission of the Editorial Committee of the Archives:

Trinity College,
Cambridge
5 Feb. 1915

MY DEAR WITTGENSTEIN,

It was a *very* great happiness to hear from you – I had been thinking of you constantly and longing for news. I am amazed that you have been able to write a MS on logic since the war began. I cannot tell you how great a joy it will be to see you again after the war, if all goes well. If only your MSS come to me, I will do my utmost to understand them and make others understand them; but without your help it will be difficult.

Your letter came about 3 weeks ago – I did not know how I should answer it, but I am enabled to by the kindness of an American who is going to Italy.

Please remember me to your mother, and tell her that you are constantly in my mind with anxious affection.

Ever yours

BERTRAND RUSSELL

R.*31*   K.u.K. Werkstätte der Festung Krakau
                              Feldpost No 186
                                   22.5.15.
Lieber Russell!

Erhielt heute Deinen lieben Brief vom 10.5. Dziewicki werde ich so bald als möglich besuchen; bin schon sehr neugierig auf ihn.

Daß Du Moores Aufschreibungen nicht hast verstehen können tut mir außerordentlich leid! Ich fühle, daß sie ohne weitere Erklärung sehr schwer verständlich sind, aber ich halte sie doch im Wesentlichen für endgültig richtig. Was ich in der letzten Zeit geschrieben habe wird nun, wie ich fürchte, noch unverständlicher sein; und, wenn ich das Ende dieses Krieges nicht mehr erlebe, so muß ich mich darauf gefaßt machen, daß meine ganze Arbeit verloren geht. – Dann soll mein Manuskript gedruckt werden, ob es irgend einer versteht, oder nicht! –

Die Probleme werden immer lapidarer und allgemeiner und die Methode hat sich durchgreifend geändert. –

Hoffen wir auf ein Wiedersehen nach dem Krieg! Sei herzlichst gegrüßt von

Deinem treuen

Ludwig Wittgenstein

(R.*31 English Translation*)

Dear Russell,

Received today your kind letter of 10.5. I will visit Dziewicki as soon as possible; I'm already very curious about him.

I'm extremely sorry that you weren't able to understand Moore's notes. I feel that they're very hard to understand without further explanation, but I regard them essentially as definitive. And now I'm afraid that what I've written recently will be still more incomprehensible, and if I don't live to see the end of this war I must be prepared for all my work to go for nothing. – In that case you must get my manuscript printed whether anyone understands it or not. –

The problems are becoming more and more lapidary and general and the method has changed drastically. –

Let's hope for a reunion after the war! Warmest regards from

Your devoted friend

LUDWIG WITTGENSTEIN

K.u.K. – Kaiserliche und Königliche (Imperial and Royal).

Dziewicki. – The reference is to M. H. Dziewicki of Cracow, who had published a paper on scholastic philosophy in the Proceedings of the Aristotelian Society. He was in philosophical correspondence with Russell during this period and in a letter to him after the war he wrote:

"I am glad . . . to get news of Wittgenstein; a most genial young man, whom I was very much pleased to meet. Will you tell him how much I rejoice to know that his gloomy forebodings have not been realized."

Against the last sentence Russell added a note: "(He expected to be killed in Russia.)"

The letter is now in the Bertrand Russell Archives and is quoted here with the kind permission of the Editorial Committee of the Archives.

R.*32*

> Frau Elsa Gröger
> Gut Wangensbach
> Küsnacht (Zch.)
> 22.10.15.

LIEBER RUSSELL!

Ich habe in der letzten Zeit sehr viel gearbeitet und, wie ich glaube, mit gutem Erfolg. Ich bin jetzt dabei das Ganze zusammenzufassen und in Form einer Abhandlung niederzuschreiben. Ich werde nun keinesfalls etwas veröffentlichen, ehe Du es gesehen hast. Das kann aber natürlich erst nach dem Kriege geschehen. Aber, wer weiß, ob ich das erleben werde. Falls ich es nicht mehr erlebe, so laß Dir von meinen Leuten meine ganzen Manuscripte schicken, darunter befindet sich auch die letzte Zusammenfassung mit Bleistift auf losen Blättern geschrieben. Es wird Dir vielleicht einige Mühe machen alles zu verstehen, aber laß Dich dadurch nicht abschrecken. Meine gegenwärtige Adresse ist:

> K.u.K. Artillerie Werkstätten Zug No 1
> Feldpost No 12.

Hast Du Pinsent in der letzten Zeit einmal gesehen? Wenn Du Johnson siehst so grüße ihn bestens von mir. Ich denke noch immer gerne an ihn und an unsere fruchtlosen und aufgeregten Disputationen. Möge der Himmel geben, daß wir uns noch einmal sehen!

Sei herzlichst gegrüßt von

> Deinem treuen
>
> WITTGENSTEIN

(R.*32 English Translation*)

DEAR RUSSELL,

I have recently done a great deal of work and, I think, quite successfully. I'm now in the process of summarizing it all and writing it down in the form of a treatise. Now: whatever happens I won't publish anything until you have seen it. But, of course, that can't happen until after the war. But who knows whether I shall survive until then? If I don't survive, get my people to send you all my manuscripts: among them you'll find the final summary written in pencil on loose sheets of paper. It will perhaps cost you some trouble to understand it all, but don't let yourself be put off by that. My present address is:

K.u.K. Artillerie Werkstätten Zug No 1
Feldpost No 12

Have you seen anything of Pinsent recently? If you see Johnson, please give him my best regards. I still remember him with great pleasure, as also the fruitless and heated discussions we used to have. Heaven grant that we may meet again sometime!

Warmest regards from

Your devoted friend

WITTGENSTEIN

Frau Elsa Gröger. Gut Wangensbach. Küsnacht (Zch.). – The address is *stamped* on the envelope and the sheet on which Wittgenstein wrote his letter. Küsnacht is in Switzerland, near Zürich. Wittgenstein presumably sent his letter to Frau Gröger, who forwarded it to England.

Johnson. – See comment to K.14.

R.*33*
Postcard

Cassino
Provincia Caserta
Italia
9.2.19.

DEAR RUSSELL,

I don't know your precise address but hope these lines will reach you somehow. I am prisoner in Italy since November and hope I may communicate with you after a three years interruption. I have done lots of logical work which I am dying to let you know before publishing it.

Ever yours

LUDWIG WITTGENSTEIN

precise address. – The postcard was addressed by Wittgenstein to Russell c/o Dr A. N. Whitehead, University College, London.

R.*34*
Postcard

Cassino
Prov[incia] Caserta
Italia
10.3.19.

You can't imagine how glad I was to get your cards! I am afraid
though there is no hope that we may meet before long. Unless you
came to see me here, but this would be too much joy for me. I
can't write on Logic as I'm not allowed to write more than 2 cards
(15 lines each) a week. I've written a book which will be published as soon as I get home. I think I have solved our problems
finally. Write to me often. It will shorten my prison. God bless
you.

Ever yours
WITTGENSTEIN

R.35   [Cassino, Provincia Caserta, Italy]
                                        13.3.19.

DEAR RUSSELL,

Thanks so much for your postcards dated 2nd and 3rd of March. I've had a *very* bad time, not knowing whether you were dead or alive! I can't write on Logic as I'm not allowed to write more than two p[ost] c[ard]s a week (15 lines each). This letter is an exception, it's posted by an Austrian medical student who goes home tomorrow. I've written a book called "Logisch-Philosophische Abhandlung" containing all my work of the last six years. I believe I've solved our problems finally. This may sound arrogant but I can't help believing it. I finished the book in August 1918 and two months after was made Prigioniere. I've got the manuscript here with me. I wish I could copy it out for you; but it's pretty long and I would have no safe way of sending it to you. In fact you would not understand it without a previous explanation as it's written in quite short remarks. (This of course means that *nobody* will understand it; although I believe, it's all as clear as crystal. But it upsets all our theory of truth, of classes, of numbers and all the rest.) I will publish it as soon as I get home. Now I'm afraid this *won't* be "before long". And consequently it will be a long time yet till we can meet. I can hardly imagine seeing you again! It will be too much! I suppose it would be impossible for you to come and see me here? or perhaps you think it's colossal cheek of me even to think of such a thing. But if you were on the other end of the world and I *could* come to you I would do it.

Please write to me how you are, remember me to Dr Whitehead. Is old Johnson still alive? Think of me often!

Ever yours

LUDWIG WITTGENSTEIN

Russell, upon receipt of this letter, copied it out by hand and had copies typed out. It is not known what he planned to do with the copies. Six of them he seems to have kept for himself; they are now in the Bertrand Russell Archives. One typed copy of the letter is in the Wittgenstein file of the Keynes Papers in King's College, Cambridge.

R.*36*   Cassino
                                                        12.6.19.
LIEBER RUSSELL!

Vor einigen Tagen schickte ich Dir mein Manuskript durch Keynes's Vermittelung. Ich schrieb damals nur ein paar Zeilen für Dich hinein. Seither ist nun Dein Buch ganz in meine Hände gelangt und nun hätte ich ein großes Bedürfnis Dir einiges zu schreiben. – Ich hätte nicht geglaubt, daß das, was ich vor 6 Jahren in Norwegen dem Moore diktierte an Dir so spurlos vorübergehen würde. Kurz ich fürchte jetzt, es möchte sehr schwer für mich sein mich mit Dir zu verständigen. Und der geringe Rest von Hoffnung mein M.S. könne Dir etwas sagen, ist ganz verschwunden. Einen Kommentar zu meinem Buch zu schreiben, bin ich, wie Du Dir denken kannst, nicht im Stande. Nur mündlich könnte ich Dir einen geben. Ist Dir irgend an dem Verständnis der Sache etwas gelegen und kannst Du ein Zusammentreffen mit mir bewerkstelligen, so bitte, tue es. – Ist dies nicht möglich, so sei so gut und schicke das M.S. so bald Du es gelesen hast auf sicherem Wege nach Wien zurück. Es ist das einzige korrigierte Exemplar, welches ich besitze und die Arbeit meines Lebens! Mehr als je brenne ich *jetzt* darauf es gedruckt zu sehen. Es ist bitter, das vollendete Werk in der Gefangenschaft herumschleppen zu müßen und zu sehen, wie der Unsinn draußen sein Spiel treibt! Und ebenso bitter ist es zu denken daß niemand es verstehen wird, auch wenn es gedruckt sein wird! – Hast Du mir jemals seit Deinen zwei ersten Karten geschrieben? Ich habe nichts erhalten.

Sei herzlichst gegrüßt und *glaube nicht, daß alles Dummheit ist was Du nicht verstehen wirst.*

                                            Dein treuer

                                            LUDWIG WITTGENSTEIN

(R.*36 English Translation*)

DEAR RUSSELL,

Some days ago I sent you my manuscript through Keynes's intermediacy. At that time I enclosed only a couple of lines for you. Since then your book has reached me *in toto* and I'd very much like to write some things to you. – I should never have believed that the stuff I dictated to Moore in Norway six years ago would have passed over you so completely without trace. In short, I'm now afraid that it might be very difficult for me to reach any understanding with you. And the small remaining hope that my manuscript might mean something to you has completely vanished. As you can imagine, I'm in no position to write a commentary on my book. I could only give you one orally. If you attach any importance whatsoever to understanding the thing and if you can manage to arrange a meeting with me, then please do so. – If that isn't possible, then be so good as to send the manuscript back to Vienna by a safe route as soon as you've read it. It is the only corrected copy I possess and is my life's work! *Now* more than ever I'm burning to see it in print. It's galling to have to lug the completed work round in captivity and to see how nonsense has a clear field outside! And it's equally galling to think that no one will understand it even if it does get printed! – Have you written to me at all since your first two postcards? I've received nothing.

Warmest regards and *don't think that everything that you won't understand is a piece of stupidity.*

Your devoted friend

Ludwig Wittgenstein

ein paar Zeilen. – These lines evidently are no longer extant.

Dein Buch ["your book"]. – Russell's *Introduction to Mathematical Philosophy*, which was published in March 1919. In a letter to J. M. Keynes of 23 March 1919 Russell says that he wanted to send his "new book" to Wittgenstein but that he does not know whether this will be possible. He also says that he had written to George Trevelyan asking him whether he could do anything to obtain permission for Wittgenstein to "communicate freely about logic". Russell wonders whether Keynes could "speak to anybody about him" and concludes the letter by saying "I wish he could get permission to come to England". Trevelyan did obtain, through Dr Filippo de Filippi, permission for Wittgenstein to receive books. Filippi recommended sending them by letter post and it seems that this book was sent in parts (*ist . . . ganz in meine Hände gelangt* ["has reached me *in toto*"]). There was some residual difficulty about letters, which perhaps accounts for the fact that Wittgenstein sent his typescript to Russell through Keynes (cf. K.9).

R.*37*   Cassino
                                                                19.8.19.

DEAR RUSSELL,

Thanks so much for your letter dated 13 August. As to your queries, I can't answer them *now*. For firstly I don't know always what the numbers refer to, having no copy of the M.S. here. Secondly some of your questions want a very lengthy answer and you know how difficult it is for me to write on logic. That's also the reason why my book is so short, and consequently so obscure. But that I can't help. – Now I'm afraid you haven't really got hold of my main contention, to which the whole business of logical prop[osition]s is only a corollary. The main point is the theory of what can be expressed (gesagt) by prop[osition]s – i.e. by language – (and, which comes to the same, what can be *thought*) and what can not be expressed by prop[osition]s, but only shown (gezeigt); which, I believe, is the cardinal problem of philosophy. – I also sent my M.S. to Frege. He wrote to me a week ago and I gather that he doesn't understand a word of it all. So my only hope is to see *you* soon and explain all to you, for it is VERY hard not to be understood by a single soul!

Now the day after tomorrow we shall probably leave the Campo Concentramento and go home. Thank God! – But how can we meet as soon as possible? I should like to come to England, but you can imagine that it's rather awkward for a German to travel to England now. (By far more so, than for an Englishman to travel to Germany.) But in fact I didn't think of asking you to come to Vienna now, but it would seem to me the best thing to meet in Holland or Switzerland. Of course, if you can't come abroad I will do my best to get to England. Please write to me as soon as possible about this point, letting me know when you are likely to get the permission of coming abroad. Please write to Vienna IV. Alleegasse 16. As to my M.S., please send it to the same address; but only if there is an absolutely safe way of sending it. Otherwise please keep it. I should be very glad though, to get it soon, as it's the only corrected copy I've got. – My mother wrote to me, she was very sorry not to have got your letter, but glad that you tried to write to her at all.

Now write soon. Best wishes.

Ever yours

LUDWIG WITTGENSTEIN

P.S. After having finished my letter I feel tempted after all to answer some of your simpler points:

(1) "What is the difference between Tatsache and Sachverhalt?" Sachverhalt is, what corresponds to an Elementarsatz if it is true. Tatsache is what corresponds to the logical product of elementary prop[osition]s when this product is true. The reason why I introduce *Tatsache* before introducing *Sachverhalt* would want a long explanation.

(2) ". . . But a Gedanke is a Tatsache: what are its constituents and components, and what is their relation to those of the pictured Tatsache?" I don't know *what* the constituents of a thought are but I know *that* it must have such constituents which correspond to the words of Language. Again the kind of relation of the constituents of thought and of the pictured fact is irrelevant. It would be a matter of psychology to find it out.

(3) "The theory of types, in my view, is a theory of correct symbolism: (a) a simple symbol must not be used to express anything complex; (b) more generally, a symbol must have the same structure as its meaning." That's exactly what one can't say. You cannot prescribe to a symbol what it *may* be used to express. All that a symbol CAN express, it MAY express. This is a short answer but it is true!

(4) Does a Gedanke consist of words? No! But of psychical constituents that have the same sort of relation to reality as words. What those constituents are I don't know.

(5) "It is awkward to be unable to speak of Nc'$\overline{V}$." This touches the cardinal question of what can be expressed by a prop[osition], and what can't be expressed, but only shown. I can't explain it at length here. Just think that, what you want to *say* by the apparent prop[osition] "there are 2 things" is *shown* by there being

two names which have different meanings (or by there being one name which may have two meanings). A prop[osition] e.g. φ(a, b) or (∃φ, x, y).φ(x, y) doesn't say that there are two things, it says something quite different; *but whether it's true or false, it* SHOWS what you want to *express* by saying: "there are 2 things".

(6) Of course no elementary prop[osition]s are negative.

(7) "It is necessary also to be given the prop[osition] that all elementary prop[osition]s are given." This is not necessary, because it is even *impossible*. There is no such prop[osition]! That all elementary prop[osition]s are given is SHOWN by there being none having an elementary sense which is not given. This is again the same story as in No 5.

(8) I suppose you didn't understand the way, how I separate in the old notation of generality what is in it truth-function and what is purely generality. A general prop[osition] is A truth-function of *all* PROP[OSITION]s of a certain form.

(9) You are quite right in saying that "N($\bar{\xi}$)" may also be made to mean ∼p ∨ ∼q ∨ ∼r ∨ ∼ .... But this doesn't matter! I suppose you don't understand the notation of "$\bar{\xi}$". It does not mean "for all values of ξ ...". But all is said in my book about it and I feel unable to write it again. Try to understand it till we meet. I never thought I could write such long explanations as I've done now.

Ever yours,

L.W.

R.*38*   Wien XVII.
                                                           Neuwaldeggerstr[aße] 38
                                                           30.8.19.

LIEBER RUSSELL!

Verzeih', daß ich Dich mit einer dummen Bitte belästige: Ich
bin jetzt mit einer Kopie meines M.S.s zu einem Verleger gegangen, um den Druck endlich in die Wege zu leiten. Der Verleger, der natürlich weder meinen Namen kennt, noch etwas von
Philosophie versteht, verlangt das Urteil irgend eines Fachmanns,
um sicher zu sein, daß das Buch wirklich wert ist, gedruckt zu
werden. Er wollte sich deshalb an einen seiner Vertrauensmänner
hier wenden (wahrscheinlich an einen Philosophie-Professor).
Ich sagte ihm, nun, daß hier niemand das Buch beurteilen könne,
daß *Du* aber vielleicht so gut sein würdest, ihm ein kurzes Urteil
über den Wert der Arbeit zu schreiben; was, wenn es günstig aus-
fällt, ihm genügen wird um den Verlag zu übernehmen. Die
Adresse des Verlegers ist: Wilhelm Braumüller. XI. Servitengasse 5 Wien. Ich bitte Dich nun, dorthin ein paar Worte, so viel
Du vor Deinem Gewissen verantworten kannst, zu schreiben.

Auch an mich schreib, bitte, recht bald! Wie es Dir geht, wann
Du auf den Continent kommen kannst, etc., etc. Wie Du siehst
bin ich aus der Gefangenschaft zurück, ich bin aber doch noch
nicht ganz normal. Aber das wird schon kommen. Sei herzlichst
gegrüßt!

                                                          Dein treuer

                                                   LUDWIG WITTGENSTEIN

(R.*38 English Translation*)

DEAR RUSSELL,

Forgive me if I burden you with a tiresome request. I've now
been to a publisher with a copy of my manuscript in order to get
its printing finally under way. The publisher, who naturally
neither knows my name nor understands anything about philosophy, requires the judgment of some expert in order to be sure
that the book is really worth printing. For this purpose he wanted

to apply to one of the people he relies on here (probably a professor of philosophy). So I told him that no one here would be able to form a judgment on the book, but that *you* would perhaps be kind enough to write him a brief assessment of the value of the work, and if this happened to be favourable that would be enough to induce him to publish it. The publisher's address is: Wilhelm Braumüller, XI Servitengasse 5, Vienna. Now please write him a few words – as much as your conscience will allow you to.

Please write to me too, very soon – how you are, when you can come to the continent, etc., etc. As you can see, I'm back from prison-camp. I'm not quite normal yet, though. But that will come soon enough. Warmest regards.

Your devoted friend
LUDWIG WITTGENSTEIN

R.*39*   6.10.19.

LIEBER RUSSELL!

Herzlichen Dank für Deinen Brief vom 12.9. Auch mein Verleger hat schon längst Dein Empfehlungsschreiben bekommen,
hat mir aber noch immer nicht geschrieben, ob, und unter welchen
Bedingungen, er mein Buch nimmt (der Hund!). Ich glaube
bestimmt zu Weihnachten in den Haag kommen zu können. Nur
ein unvorsehbares Ereignis könnte mich daran hindern. Ich habe
mich entschlossen Lehrer zu werden und muß dazu noch einmal
eine sogenannte Lehrerbildungsanstalt besuchen. Dort sitzen
lauter Buben von 17–18 Jahren und ich bin schon 30. Das giebt
sehr komische Situationen und oft auch *sehr* unangenehme. Ich
fühle mich oft unglücklich! – Mit Frege stehe ich in Briefwechsel.
Er versteht kein Wort von meiner Arbeit und ich bin schon ganz
erschöpft vor lauter Erklärungen.

Wie geht es Dr Whitehead und Johnson? Schreibe bald.

Dein treuer

LUDWIG WITTGENSTEIN

P.S. Wann kannst Du mir voraussichtlich mein M.S. zurückschicken? Meine Adresse ist jetzt:

Wien III., Untere Viaduktgasse 9 bei Frau Wanicek

Aber auch Briefe an meine alte Adresse erreichen mich. Ich wohne
nämlich nicht mehr bei meiner Mutter. Ich habe mein ganzes
Geld weggeschenkt und werde bald versuchen, mir selbst etwas
zu verdienen. *Oft* denke ich an Dich!

L.W.

(R.*39 English Translation*)

DEAR RUSSELL,

Warmest thanks for your letter of 12.9. My publisher too received your testimonial long ago but has still not written to me to
say whether and under what conditions he will take my book (the

swine!). I think I'll *certainly* be able to come to The Hague at Christmastime. Only some unpredictable occurrence could prevent me. I have made up my mind to become a teacher and so must go back to school at a so-called Teachers' Training College. The benches are full of boys of 17 or 18 and I've reached 30. That leads to some very funny situations – and many *very* unpleasant ones too. I often feel miserable! – I'm in correspondence with Frege. He doesn't understand a single word of my work and I'm thoroughly exhausted from giving what are purely and simply explanations.

How are Dr Whitehead and Johnson? Write soon.

Your devoted friend,

LUDWIG WITTGENSTEIN

P.S. When do you think you can send me back by MS? My address now is:

Vienna III., Untere Viaduktgasse 9 bei Frau Wanicek

but letters to my old address will also reach me. The fact is, I'm not living at my mother's any more. I've given all my money away and am shortly going to try to earn something for myself. I think of you *often*!

L.W.

R.*40*   1.11.19.

LIEBER RUSSELL!

Ich besorge mir jetzt den Paß für Holland und werde Dich am 10ten Dezember im Haag treffen. Mit dem Geld hat es allerdings eine gewisse Schwierigkeit; eine Woche wird mich aber auf keinen Fall umbringen. – Nun habe ich aber eine Idee, weiß allerdings nicht, ob sie durchführbar ist: Ich habe nämlich seinerzeit, als ich von Cambridge nach Norwegen gezogen bin, alle meine Sachen in Cambridge bei einem Möbelhändler deponiert (seinen Namen habe ich vergessen, es war nicht der Lilies sondern einer in der Nähe von Magdalene College). Es waren viele Bücher, darunter auch ein paar wertvolle, ein Teppich, etc. *Sind nun alle diese Sachen schon verfallen?* Wenn nicht, so hätte ich eine große Bitte an Dich: nämlich, sie zu verkaufen und mir das Geld nach Holland mitzubringen. Bitte sei so gut und schreibe mir, ob das überhaupt möglich ist.

Ich freue mich unbeschreiblich auf unser Wiedersehen.

Sei herzlichst gegrüßt von Deinem treuen

LUDWIG WITTGENSTEIN

Meine Adresse ist jetzt: Wien, XIII, St. Veitgasse 17
bei Frau Sjögren.

Hast Du schon das M.S. abgeschickt?

L.W.

P.P.S. Etwas ÄUSSERST WICHTIGES fällt mir ein: Unter meinen Sachen befinden sich auch eine Menge Tagebücher und Manuscripte diese sind ALLE zu verbrennen!!!

(R.*40 English Translation*)

DEAR RUSSELL,

I am now getting my passport for Holland and will meet you in The Hague on 10 December. Sure enough there are certain difficulties over money but whatever happens a week won't kill me. – A thought occurs to me, however, though I don't know whether it's practicable. The thing is that at the time I moved

from Cambridge to Norway, I stored all my things in Cambridge
at a furniture dealer's. (I've forgotten his name. It wasn't Lilies
but one near Magdalene College.) There were a good few books,
including a couple of valuable ones, a carpet, etc. *Now*: *have I lost
all claim to these things?* If not, then I'd like to ask a great favour of
you – i.e. to sell them and to bring the money to Holland for me.
Please be so good as to write to me if this is at all possible.

I look forward more than I can say to our meeting.

Warmest regards from your devoted friend

LUDWIG WITTGENSTEIN

My address now is: Vienna XIII, St Veitgasse 17
bei Frau Sjögren.

Have you sent the MS yet?

P.P.S. Something EXTREMELY IMPORTANT has just occurred to me.
Among my things there are a lot of journal-notebooks and manuscripts. These are ALL to be burnt!!!

Möbelhändler ["furniture dealer"]. – The dealer was B. Jolley &
Sons. Russell bought the books and the furniture ("the best bargain I
ever made" he says in his *Autobiography* II, p. 100). Some at least of the
books are still in Russell's library and will in due course join the Russell Archives at McMaster University.

R.*41*   21.11.19.

LIEBER RUSSELL!

Heute erhielt ich das M.S. Vielen Dank. Ich habe es bisher nur flüchtig durchgesehen und nur zwei Bemerkungen von Deiner Hand gefunden. Über alles werden wir sprechen, wenn wir uns im Haag treffen. Meinen Pass habe ich bereits und die Einreisebe- willigung von Holland werde ich hoffentlich auch bekommen. Ich kann es schon gar nicht mehr erwarten, Dich zu sehen. Hast Du meinen letzten Brief erhalten? Ich bat Dich in ihm meine Sachen in Cambridge, falls sie noch existieren, zu verkaufen und mir den Erlös mit nach Holland zu bringen, da ich mit dem Geld einige Schwierigkeiten habe.

Bitte schreibe bald. Meine Adresse ist: Wien XIII, St. Veit- gasse 17 bei Frau Sjögren.

Sei herzlichst gegrüßt

von Deinem treuen

LUDWIG WITTGENSTEIN

(R.*41 English Translation*)

DEAR RUSSELL,

I received the MS today. Many thanks. So far I've only leafed through it and only found two remarks in your handwriting. We shall talk about everything when we meet in The Hague. I have my passport already and hope to get the Dutch entry-permit also. Already I can hardly wait to see you. Did you get my last letter? In it I asked you to sell my things in Cambridge, if they still exist, and to bring the proceeds to Holland for me, because I have some difficulties with money.

Please write soon. My address is: Vienna XIII, St Veitgasse 17 bei Frau Sjögren.

Warmest regards from your devoted friend

LUDWIG WITTGENSTEIN

R.*42*   Wien XIII
                                   St. Veitgasse 17 bei Frau Sjögren
                                          27.11.19.

LIEBER RUSSELL!

Dank' Dir bestens für Deinen Brief. Wenn Du nur in den Haag
kommen kannst! Bitte TELEGRAPHIERE mir sofort wenn Du es
weißt, da ich bereits den Pass habe und angab, daß ich vom 13ten–
20ten im Haag zu sein beabsichtige. Eine neuerliche Änderung des
Termins würde große Schwierigkeiten machen. Also bitte, laß
mich nicht auf Deine Nachricht warten! – Mit dem Möbelhändler
hast Du ganz recht, es ist Jolley. Ich glaube aber, er wird schon
Deine Bevollmächtigung anerkennen. –

Ich habe jetzt erneute Schwierigkeiten wegen meines Buches.
Niemand will es verlegen. Erinnerst Du Dich noch, wie Du mich
immer drängtest etwas zu veröffentlichen: und jetzt, wo ich es
möchte, geht es nicht. Das soll der Teufel holen!

Wann immer Du in den Haag kommst, laß, bitte, Deine Adresse auf der Österreichischen Gesandtschaft. Dort werde ich sie
erfahren.

Sei herzlichst gegrüßt von Deinem immer
                                             treuen
                                    LUDWIG WITTGENSTEIN

(R.42 English Translation)

DEAR RUSSELL,

Thank you very much for your letter. If only you are able to
come to The Hague! Please WIRE me immediately you know because I've got my passport already and have stated my intention
of being in The Hague from the 13th to the 20th. A new change of
date would give rise to great difficulties. So please don't keep me
waiting for your news! – You're quite right about the furniture
dealer. It is Jolley. But I think he'll be satisfied with the authority
you've got. –

The difficulties with my book have started up again. Nobody
wants to publish it. Do you remember how you were always
pressing me to publish something? And now when I should like
to, it can't be managed. The devil take it!

Whenever you do arrive in The Hague, please leave your address at the Austrian Legation. I'll find it there.
Warmest regards from your devoted friend

as ever

LUDWIG WITTGENSTEIN

About his encounter with Wittgenstein Russell wrote to Lady Ottoline from The Hague on 20 December:

I have much to tell you that is of interest. I leave here today, after a fortnight's stay, during a week of which Wittgenstein was here, and we discussed his book every day. I came to think even better of it than I had done; I feel sure it is a really great book, though I do not feel sure it is right. I told him I could not refute it, and that I was sure it was either all right or all wrong, which I considered the mark of a good book; but it would take me years to decide this. This of course didn't satisfy him, but I couldn't say more.

I had felt in his book a flavour of mysticism, but was astonished when I found that he has become a complete mystic. He reads people like Kierkegaard and Angelus Silesius, and he seriously contemplates becoming a monk. It all started from William James's Varieties of Religious Experience, and grew (not unnaturally) during the winter he spent alone in Norway before the war, when he was nearly mad. Then during the war a curious thing happened. He went on duty to the town of Tarnov in Galicia, and happened to come upon a bookshop, which, however, seemed to contain nothing but picture postcards. However, he went inside and found that it contained just one book: Tolstoy on The Gospels. He bought it merely because there was no other. He read it and re-read it, and thenceforth had it always with him, under fire and at all times. But on the whole he likes Tolstoy less than Dostoewski (especially Karamazov). He has penetrated deep into mystical ways of thought and feeling, but I think (though he wouldn't agree) that what he likes best in mysticism is its power to make him stop thinking. I don't much think he will really become a monk – it is an idea, not an intention. His intention is to be a teacher. He gave all his money to his brothers and sisters, because he found earthly possessions a burden. I wish you had seen him.

. . .

R.*43*   Wien XIII
                                                        St. Veitgasse 17
                                                        8.1.20.

LIEBER RUSSELL!

Herzlichen Dank für Deine Bücher; sie werden mich beide in-
teressieren. Wenige Tage nach meiner Ankunft in Wien wurde ich
krank, aber jetzt geht es schon wieder. Von meinen vorhabenden
Verlegern habe ich noch keine Antwort auf die Mitteilung, daß
Du meinem Buch mit einer Einleitung nachhelfen willst. Sobald
ich etwas erfahre, schreibe ich Dir.

Wie geht es Dir? Bist Du in Cambridge?

Ich habe unser Beisammensein *sehr* genossen und ich habe das
Gefühl daß wir in dieser Woche sehr viel wirklich gearbeitet
haben. (Du nicht auch?)

Sei vielmals gegrüßt

von Deinem treuen

LUDWIG WITTGENSTEIN

(R.*43 English Translation*)

DEAR RUSSELL,

Many thanks for your books. Both of them will be interesting
for me. A few days after arriving in Vienna I fell ill but now I'm
more or less all right again. I've still no answer from my various
prospective publishers to the information that you're willing to
come to the aid of my book with an introduction. As soon as I
hear anything, I'll write to you.

How are you? Are you in Cambridge?

I enjoyed our time together *very* much and I have the feeling
(haven't you too?) that we did a great deal of real work during
that week.

Best regards from your devoted friend

LUDWIG WITTGENSTEIN

Deine Bücher ["your books"]. – The letter makes reference to *two*
books. It is a reasonable conjecture that they were *Our Knowledge of the
External World* and the collection of essays *Mysticism and Logic*.

in Cambridge. – Russell was living in London at this time.

R.*44*   Wien XIII
                                    St. Veitgasse 17 bei Frau Sjögren
                                    19.1.20.

LIEBER RUSSELL!

Heute erhielt ich die Nachricht, daß der Verlag von Reclam in
Leipzig aller Wahrscheinlichkeit nach mein Buch nehmen will.
Ich werde also mein M.S. aus Innsbruck kommen lassen und es
an Reclam schicken. Wann aber kommt Deine Einleitung?! Denn
ohne sie kann ja der Druck nicht beginnen. *Wenn* Du also gewillt
bist, sie zu schreiben, so bitte tue es so bald als möglich und lasse
mich wissen ob, und wann ich Dein M.S. erwarten darf. Ich ve-
getiere hier ohne viel Freude am Leben. Schreib mir bald.

                            Dein treuer

                                    LUDWIG WITTGENSTEIN

(R.*44 English Translation*)

DEAR RUSSELL,

I have had word today that the Leipzig publisher Reclam is prepared, in all probability, to take my book. So I will get my MS
sent from Innsbruck and will forward it to Reclam. But when is
your introduction going to arrive?! Because the printing can't
begin without it. So: *if* you're prepared to write it, please do so as
soon as possible and let me know whether and when I can expect
your MS. I am vegetating here and not enjoying life very much.
Write to me soon.

                        Your devoted friend

                                    LUDWIG WITTGENSTEIN

R.45   19.3.20.

LIEBER RUSSELL!

Es ist lange her seit Du von mir gehört hast. Wie steht's mit der Einleitung? Ist sie schon fertig? Und wie geht es mit Deinem Schlüsselbein, wie hast Du es Dir denn gebrochen? Wie gern möchte ich Dich wieder sehen. Ich bin nicht mehr im Stande mir neue Freunde zu erwerben und die alten verliere ich. Das ist schrecklich traurig. Fast täglich denke ich an den armen David Pinsent. Denn, so sonderbar das klingt, ich bin fast allen Menschen zu dumm!

Schreib mir bald einmal und schicke auch Deine Einleitung.

Dein trauriger

LUDWIG WITTGENSTEIN

(R.45 *English Translation*)

DEAR RUSSELL,

It is a very long time since you heard from me. How are things with the introduction? Is it finished yet? And how is your collarbone? How did you manage to break it? How much I'd like to see you again! I'm no longer in any condition to acquire new friends and I'm losing my old ones. It's terribly sad. Nearly every day I remember poor David Pinsent. Because, however odd it sounds, I'm too stupid for nearly everybody.

Do write to me soon and also send your introduction.

Your sad friend

LUDWIG WITTGENSTEIN

R.*46*   9.4.20.

LIEBER RUSSELL!

Besten Dank für Dein Manuscript. Ich bin mit so manchem darin nicht ganz einverstanden; sowohl dort, wo Du mich kritisierst, als auch dort, wo Du bloß meine Ansicht klarlegen willst. Das macht aber nichts. Die Zukunft wird über uns urteilen. Oder auch nicht – und wenn sie schweigen wird, so wird das auch ein Urteil sein. – Die Einleitung wird jetzt übersetzt und geht dann mit der Abhandlung zum Verleger. Hoffentlich nimmt er sie! – Hier gibt es wenig Neues. Ich bin so dumm wie gewöhnlich. Meine Adresse ist jetzt: Wien III. Rasumofskygasse 24 (bei Herrn Zimmermann). Sei herzlichst gegrüßt!

Dein treuer

LUDWIG WITTGENSTEIN

(R.*46 English Translation*)

DEAR RUSSELL,

Thank you very much for your manuscript. There's so much of it that I'm not quite in agreement with – both where you're critical of me and also where you're simply trying to elucidate my point of view. But that doesn't matter. The future will pass judgment on us – or perhaps it won't, and if it is silent that will be a judgment too. – The introduction is in the course of being translated and will then go with the treatise to the publisher. I hope he will accept them! – There's nothing much new here. I am as stupid as usual. My address is now: Vienna III., Rasumofskygasse 24 (bei Herrn Zimmermann). Warmest regards from your devoted friend

LUDWIG WITTGENSTEIN

R.*47*   6.5.20.

LIEBER RUSSELL!

Sei für Deinen lieben Brief herzlich bedankt. Nun wirst Du aber auf mich böse sein, wenn ich Dir etwas erzähle: Deine Einleitung wird nicht gedruckt und infolgedessen wahrscheinlich auch mein Buch nicht. – Als ich nämlich die deutsche Übersetzung der Einleitung vor mir hatte, da konnte ich mich doch nicht entschließen sie mit meiner Arbeit drucken zu lassen. Die Feinheit Deines englischen Stils war nämlich in der Übersetzung – selbstverständlich – verloren gegangen und was übrig blieb war Oberflächlichkeit und Mißverständnis. Ich schickte nun die Abhandlung und Deine Einleitung an Reclam und schrieb ihm, ich wünschte nicht daß die Einleitung gedruckt würde, sondern sie solle ihm nur zur Orientierung über meine Arbeit dienen. Es ist nun höchst wahrscheinlich, daß Reclam meine Arbeit daraufhin nicht nimmt (obwohl ich noch keine Antwort von ihm habe). Aber darüber habe ich mich bereits beruhigt; und zwar mit folgendem Argument, das mir unantastbar erscheint: Meine Arbeit ist nämlich entweder ein Werk ersten Ranges, oder sie ist kein Werk ersten Ranges. Im zweiten – wahrscheinlicheren – Falle bin ich selbst dafür, daß sie nicht gedruckt werde. Und im ersten ist es ganz gleichgültig ob sie 20 oder 100 Jahre früher oder später gedruckt wird. Denn wer fragt danach ob z.B. die Kritik der reinen Vernunft im Jahre 17x oder y geschrieben worden ist! Ja, eigentlich brauchte sie in diesem Falle auch nicht gedruckt zu werden. – Und nun sei nicht bös! Es war vielleicht undankbar von mir, aber ich konnte nicht anders.

Sei herzlichst gegrüßt

von Deinem treuen
LUDWIG WITTGENSTEIN

Es wäre herrlich wenn Du im Sommer nach Wien kämst!

(R.*47 English Translation*)

DEAR RUSSELL,
Many thanks indeed for your kind letter. But now you'll be angry with me when I tell you something: Your Introduction is not going to be printed and as a consequence my book probably won't be either. – You see, when I actually saw the German translation of the Introduction, I couldn't bring myself to let it be printed with my work. All the refinement of your English style was, obviously, lost in the translation and what remained was superficiality and misunderstanding. Well, I sent the treatise with your Introduction to Reclam and wrote saying that I didn't want the Introduction printed, it was meant to serve only for his own orientation in relation to my work. It is now highly probable that as a result Reclam won't accept my work (though I've had no answer from him yet). But I've already comforted myself on that score, by means of the following argument, which seems to me unanswerable. Either my piece is a work of the highest rank, or it is not a work of the highest rank. In the latter (and more probable) case I myself am in favour of its not being printed. And in the former case it's a matter of indifference whether it's printed twenty or a hundred years sooner or later. After all, who asks whether the Critique of Pure Reason, for example, was written in 17x or y. So really in the former case too my treatise wouldn't need to be printed. – And now, don't be angry! Perhaps it was ungrateful of me but I couldn't do anything else.
Warmest regards from your devoted friend

LUDWIG WITTGENSTEIN

It would be marvellous if you could come to Vienna in the summer.

deutsche Übersetzung ["German translation"]. – This, as far as I have been able to ascertain, was *not* the translation which was eventually printed with Wittgenstein's book by Ostwald in 1921. Ostwald seems to have had another translation made from Russell's English original. Cf. *Prototractatus*, Historical Introduction, pp. 28–29.

R.*48*   Wien III
                                                  Rasumofskygasse 24/II
                                                  bei Herrn Zimmermann
                                                  7.7.20.
LIEBER RUSSELL!

Dank Dir vielmals für Dienen lieben Brief! Reclam hat mein
Buch natürlich nicht genommen und ich werde vorläufig keine
weiteren Schritte tun, um es zu publizieren. Hast Du aber Lust es
drucken zu lassen, so steht es Dir ganz zur Verfügung und *Du
kannst damit machen, was Du willst.* (Nur wenn Du am Text etwas
änderst, so *gib an, daß die Änderung von Dir ist.*)

Heute habe ich mein Zeugnis bekommen und kann jetzt Lehrer
werden. Wie es mir gehen wird – wie ich das Leben ertragen
werde – weiß Gott allein. Am besten wäre es vielleicht, ich
könnte mich eines Abends hinlegen und nicht mehr aufwachen.
(Vielleicht aber gibt es auch noch etwas besseres für mich.) Wir
werden ja sehen. –

Sei herzlichst gegrüßt

von Deinem treuen

LUDWIG WITTGENSTEIN

(R.*48 English Translation*)

DEAR RUSSELL,

Very many thanks for your kind letter. Reclam has, naturally,
not accepted my book and for the moment I won't take any further steps to have it published. But if you feel like getting it
printed, it is entirely at your disposal and *you can do what you like
with it.* (Only, if you change anything in the text, *indicate that the
change was made by you.*)

Today I got my certificate, and I can now become a teacher.
How things will go for me – how I'll endure life – God only
knows. The best for me, perhaps, would be if I could lie down
one evening and not wake up again. (But perhaps there is something better left for me.) We shall see.

Warmest regards from your devoted friend

LUDWIG WITTGENSTEIN

mein Zeugnis ["my certificate"]. – Wittgenstein's certificate from the
teacher's training college in Vienna which he attended in the academic
year 1919–1920.

R.*49*   10.7.20.

LIEBER RUSSELL!

Eine Freundin meiner Schwester, Frau Margarethe Faber, hält sich gegenwärtig für kurze Zeit in London W, 6, Berkeley street auf. Könntest Du ihr den Inhalt jener Kassette schicken, die ich Dir, als ich nach Norwegen ging, übergab? Wenn es Dir keine Mühe macht, so, bitte, tue es. Ist aber die Kassette jetzt nicht in Deiner Hand, so macht es nichts; es wird sich schon einmal Gelegenheit bieten, die Sachen zu schicken. Wenn Du sie jetzt an Frau Faber schickst, so bitte schreibe Deinen Namen auf das Packet, damit man es Dir zurückschicken kann, im Falle Frau Faber bereits abgereist wäre.

Wenn Du wieder einmal Zeit hast, so schreib' auch Deinem

treuen

LUDWIG WITTGENSTEIN

(R.*49 English Translation*)

DEAR RUSSELL,

A lady who is a friend of my sister's, Frau Margarethe Faber, is at the moment in London (6 Berkeley St, W) for a short stay. Could you send her the contents of the casket I entrusted to you when I left for Norway? Please do this, if it's no trouble. But if the casket is not to hand at the moment, it doesn't matter. There's bound to be an opportunity to send the things sometime. If you do send them to Frau Faber now, please write your name on the parcel so that it can be sent back to you if she should already have left.

When you have time again, please also write to

Your devoted friend

LUDWIG WITTGENSTEIN

R.50　　　　　　　　　　　　　　　　　　　6.8.20.

LIEBER RUSSELL!

Vor ein paar Tagen erhielt ich eine Einladung vom Trinity
College zu einem Diner, das am 30. September stattfinden soll. Es
wurde gewiß nicht für möglich gehalten, daß ich wirklich kom-
men könnte; trotzdem hat mich die Einladung sehr gefreut.
Möchtest Du so gut sein, und in meinem Namen beim junior
Bursar absagen, da ich die Form einer solchen Absage nicht weiß.

Ich verbringe jetzt meine Ferien als Gärtnergehilfe in der Gärt-
nerei des Stiftes Klosterneuburg bei Wien. Ich muß den ganzen
Tag über fest arbeiten; und das ist gut. – Im Inneren geht es mir
nicht besonders. – Wann werden wir uns wiedersehen? Vielleicht
nie. Täglich denke ich an Pinsent. Er hat mein halbes Leben mit
sich genommen. Die andere Hälfte wird der Teufel holen. Bis
dahin bin ich immer

Dein treuer

LUDWIG WITTGENSTEIN

(R.50 English Translation)

DEAR RUSSELL,

A few days ago I received an invitation from Trinity College to
a dinner to be held on 30 September. It was surely not thought
possible that I could really come, but none the less the invitation
gave me a great deal of pleasure. Could you be so good as to
write to the Junior Bursar on my behalf declining the invitation,
because I don't know the right form for such a thing?

At the moment I'm spending my holidays as a gardener's assist-
ant in the nurseries of the monastery of Klosterneuburg near
Vienna. I have to work solidly the whole day through, which is
good. – My inner life is nothing to write home about. – When
shall we see one another again? Perhaps never. Every day I think
of Pinsent. He took half my life away with him. The devil will
take the other half. In the meantime I am, as always,

Your devoted friend

LUDWIG WITTGENSTEIN

R.*51*   20.9.20.

LIEBER RUSSELL!

Dank' Dir für Deinen lieben Brief! Ich habe jetzt eine An-
stellung bekommen; und zwar als Volksschullehrer in einem der
kleinsten Dörfer; es heißt Trattenbach und liegt 4 Stunden süd-
lich von Wien im Gebirge. Es dürfte wohl das erste mal sein, daß
der Volksschullehrer von Trattenbach mit einem Universitäts-
professor in Peking korrespondiert. Wie geht es Dir und was
trägst Du vor? Philosophie? Dann wollte ich, ich könnte zu-
hören und dann mit Dir streiten. Ich war bis vor kurzem *schrecklich bedrückt* und lebensmüde, jetzt aber bin ich etwas hoffnungs-
voller und jetzt hoffe ich auch, daß wir uns wiedersehen werden.

Gott mit Dir! Und sei herzlichst gegrüßt von Deinem

treuen

LUDWIG WITTGENSTEIN

Meine Adresse ist:

L.W. Lehrer,
Trattenbach bei Kirchberg am Wechsel
Nieder-Österreich

(R.*51 English Translation*)

DEAR RUSSELL,

Thank you for your kind letter. I have now obtained a position:
I am to be an elementary-school teacher in a tiny village called
Trattenbach. It's in the mountains, about four hours' journey
south of Vienna. It must be the first time that the schoolmaster at
Trattenbach has ever corresponded with a professor in Peking.
How are you? And what are you lecturing on? Philosophy? If so,
I wish I could attend and could argue with you afterwards. A
short while ago I was *terribly depressed* and tired of living, but now
I am slightly more hopeful, and one of the things I hope is that
we'll meet again.

God be with you! Warmest regards from

Your devoted friend

LUDWIG WITTGENSTEIN

My address is:

LW Schoolmaster
Trattenbach bei Kirchberg am Wechsel
Nieder-Österreich

Peking. – Russell had gone to China early in the autumn of 1920; he returned to England at the end of August 1921.

R.*52*   23.10.21.

LIEBER RUSSELL!

Verzeih, daß ich Dir erst jetzt auf Deinen Brief aus China antworte. Ich habe ihn sehr verspätet erhalten. Er traf mich nicht in Trattenbach und wurde mir an verschiedene Orte nachgeschickt, ohne mich zu erreichen. – Es tut mir sehr leid, daß Du krank warst; und gar schwer! *Wie geht es denn jetzt?!* Bei mir hat sich nichts verändert. Ich bin noch immer in Trattenbach und bin nach wie vor von Gehässigkeit und Gemeinheit umgeben. Es ist wahr, daß die Menschen im Durchschnitt nirgends sehr viel wert sind; aber hier sind sie viel mehr als anderswo nichtsnutzig und unverantwortlich. Ich werde vielleicht noch dieses Jahr in Trattenbach bleiben, aber länger wohl nicht, da ich mich hier auch mit den übrigen Lehrern nicht gut vertrage. (Vielleicht wird das wo anders auch nicht besser sein.) Ja, *das wäre schön*, wenn Du mich einmal besuchen wolltest. Ich bin froh zu hören, daß mein Manuskript in Sicherheit ist. Wenn es gedruckt wird, wird's mir auch recht sein. –

Schreib mir bald ein paar Zeilen, wie es Dir geht, etc., etc.

Sei herzlich gegrüßt

von Deinem treuen

LUDWIG WITTGENSTEIN

Empfiehl mich der Miss Black.

(R.*52 English Translation*)

DEAR RUSSELL,

Forgive me for only now answering your letter from China. I got it after a very long delay. I wasn't in Trattenbach when it arrived and it was forwarded to several places before it reached me. – I am very sorry that you have been ill – and seriously ill! *How are you now, then?* As regards me, nothing has changed. I am still at Trattenbach, surrounded, as ever, by odiousness and baseness. I know that human beings on the average are not worth much anywhere, but here they are much more good-for-nothing

and irresponsible than elsewhere. I will perhaps stay on in Trattenbach for the present year but probably not any longer, because I
don't get on well here even with the other teachers (perhaps that
won't be better in another place). Yes, *it would be splendid* if you
would visit me sometime. I am glad to hear that my manuscript is
in safety. And if it's printed, that will suit me too. –

    Write me a few lines soon, to say how you are, etc., etc.

Warmest regards from

your devoted friend

LUDWIG WITTGENSTEIN

Remember me to Miss Black.

Miss Black. – Dora Black, whom Russell married after their return
from the journey to China.

daß er es genau so
druckt, wie es bei mir
steht. Ich traue dem
Ostwald zu, daß er
die Arbeit nach
seinem Geschmack, etwa
nach seiner blödsinnigen
Orthographie, verändert.
Am liebsten ist es
mir, daß die Sache in
England erscheint.
Möge sie der vielen
Mühe die du und
andere mit ihr hattet

R.53   28.11.21.

LIEBER RUSSELL!

Dank Dir vielmals für Deinen lieben Brief. Ehrlich gestanden:
es freut mich, daß mein Zeug gedruckt wird. Wenn auch der Ostwald ein Erzscharlatan ist! Wenn er es nur nicht verstümmelt!
Liest Du die Korrekturen? Dann bitte sei so lieb und gib acht,
daß er es genau so druckt, wie es bei mir steht. Ich traue dem
Ostwald zu, daß er die Arbeit nach seinem Geschmack, etwa nach
seiner blödsinnigen Orthographie, verändert. Am liebsten ist es
mir, daß die Sache in England erscheint. Möge sie der vielen
Mühe die Du und andere mit ihr hatten würdig sein! –

Du hast recht: nicht die Trattenbacher allein sind schlechter, als
alle übrigen Menschen; wohl aber ist Trattenbach ein besonders
minderwertiger Ort in Österreich und die *Österreicher* sind – seit
dem Krieg – bodenlos tief gesunken, daß es zu traurig ist, davon
zu reden! So ist es. – Wenn Du diese Zeilen kriegst, ist vielleicht
schon Dein Kind auf dieser merkwürdigen Welt. Also: ich gratu-
liere Dir und Deiner Frau herzlichst. Verzeih' daß ich so lange
nicht geschrieben habe; auch ich bin etwas kränklich und riesig
beschäftigt. Bitte schreibe wieder einmal wenn Du Zeit hast. Von
Ostwald habe ich keinen Brief erhalten. Wenn alles gut geht werde
ich Dich mit tausend Freuden besuchen!

Herzlichste Grüße,

Dein

LUDWIG WITTGENSTEIN

(*R.53 English Translation*)

DEAR RUSSELL,

Many thanks for your kind letter! I must admit I am pleased
that my stuff is going to be printed. Even though Ostwald is an
utter charlatan. As long as he doesn't tamper with it! Are you
going to read the proofs? If so, please take care that he prints it
exactly as I have it. He is quite capable of altering the work to suit
his own tastes – putting it into his idiotic spelling, for example.

What pleases me most is that the whole thing is going to appear in England. I hope it may be worth all the trouble that you and others have taken with it. You are right: the Trattenbachers are not uniquely worse than the rest of the human race. But Trattenbach is a particularly insignificant place in Austria and the *Austrians* have sunk so miserably low since the war that it's too dismal to talk about. That's what it is. – By the time you get this letter your child will perhaps already have come into this remarkable world. So: warmest congratulations to you and your wife! Forgive me for not having written to you for so long. I too haven't been very well and I've been tremendously busy. Please write again when you have time. I have not had a letter from Ostwald. If all goes well, I will come and visit you with the greatest of pleasure.

Warmest regards,

Yours

LUDWIG WITTGENSTEIN

R.54   Wednesday
                                                         [July 1929]

DEAR RUSSELL,

On Saturday the 13ᵗʰ I will read a paper to the Aristotelian Society in Nottingham and I would like to ask you if you could possibly manage to come there, as your presence would improve the discussion *immensely* and perhaps would be the only thing making it worth while at all. My paper (the one *written* for the meeting) is "Some remarks on logical form", but I intend to read something else to them about generality and infinity in mathematics which, I believe, will be greater fun*. – I fear that whatever one says to them will either fall flat or arouse *irrelevant* troubles in their minds and questions and therefore I would be much obliged to you if you came, in order – as I said – to make the discussion worth while.

                                        Yours ever

                                        L. WITTGENSTEIN

*though it may be all Chinese to them.

The Joint Session of the Aristotelian Society and the Mind Association was held in University College, Nottingham 12–15 July 1929. Wittgenstein's written contribution "Some Remarks on Logical Form" was published under that title in the Supplementary Volume IX to the *Proceedings of the Aristotelian Society* for 1929, pp. 162–171.

Russell's Appointments Diary does not show that he went to Nottingham.

R.*55*   [Cambridge]
                                                          [April 1930]

DEAR RUSSELL,

Still in the motorcar to Penzance I thought of a notation I have
used in my M.S. which you can't possibly understand as – I believe – it's explained nowhere: I use the sign $\overline{\Pi}'$. Now first of all
I must say that where you find two capital I like this Π this means
Π for I had no Π on my typewriter. Now Π' is a prescription derived from the prescription Π (i.e. the prescription according to
which we develop the decimal extension of Π) by some such rule
as the following: "Whenever you meet a 7 in the decimal extension of Π, replace it by a 3" or "Whenever you get to three 5's in
that extension replace them by 2" etc. In my original M.S. I de-
noted this sort of thing by $\overset{5\rightarrow3}{\Pi}$ and I'm not sure whether I haven't
used this sign in a place of my typewritten M.S. too. – Of course
there are probably lots and lots of such details which make the
paper unintelligible, quite apart from the fact that it is unintelligible in any case. Another instance occurs to me just now: When
I write "$\underset{4}{\Pi}$" I mean Π developed to 4 places in some given system, say, the decimal system. Thus $\underset{1}{\Pi} = 3$, $\underset{2}{\Pi} = 3.1$ in the decimal
system.

I can't think of anything else to write in the moment. I feel depressed and terribly muddled in my head which is partly due to the
Cambridge climate which it always takes me several days to get
accustomed to. I feel there must be almost as many faults as words
in this letter, but I can't help it.

                                        Yours ever

                                        L. WITTGENSTEIN

The references are to one stage of the typescript which was posthumously published under its original title *Philosophische Bemerkungen*
(Basil Blackwell, Oxford 1964). Cf. also M.13. Wittgenstein composed
it during the Easter Vacation when he was in Vienna, and on his return
he gave it to Russell in Cornwall. It was on the merits of this piece of

work that Trinity College, for a second time, gave Wittgenstein a grant of £100. Russell and J. E. Littlewood had been appointed to report on it for the College Council. Russell's report is highly interesting. It is printed in full in his *Autobiography* II, p. 199 f.

R.*56*   Trinity Coll[ege]
                                          Wednesday
                                          [Academic year 1935–1936]
                                          [Presumably Autumn 1935]

DEAR RUSSELL,

Two years ago, or so, I promised you to send you a M.S. of
mine. Now the one I'm sending you today isn't *that* M.S. I'm still
pottering about with it and God knows whether I will ever publish it, or any of it. But two years ago I held some lectures in Cambridge and dictated some notes to my pupils so that they might
have something to carry home with them, in their hands if not in
their brains. And I had these notes duplicated. I have just now
been correcting misprints and other mistakes in some of the copies
and the idea came into my mind whether you might not like to
have a copy. So I'm sending you one. I don't wish to suggest that
you should read the lectures; but *if* you should have nothing better to do and *if* you should get some mild enjoyment out of them
I would be very pleased indeed. (I think it's very difficult to
understand them, as so many points are just hinted at. They were
meant only for the people who heard the lectures.) As I say, if you
don't read them *it doesn't matter at all*.

                              Yours ever

                                          LUDWIG WITTGENSTEIN

The MS. which Wittgenstein sent to Russell must have been the so-
called Blue Book. It was dictated to his class in the academic year 1933–
1934. The other piece of writing to which Wittgenstein refers here can
hardly be anything other than a typescript of 768 pages which Wittgenstein composed some time in 1932–1933 and which was a successor to
the *Philosophische Bemerkungen* of 1930. An account of this typescript is
given in the Editor's Note in *Philosophische Grammatik* (Basil Blackwell,
Oxford, 1969). Russell's copy of the Blue Book, with some corrections
and changes by the author, is now in the Russell Archives at McMaster
University.

R.*57*   Trin[ity] Coll[ege]
                                    Sunday
                                    [Presumably November 1935]

DEAR RUSSELL,

I'm in a slight difficulty: I gather that you're coming up to read
a paper to the Moral Sc[iences] Club on the 28th. Now it would be
the natural thing for me to attend the meeting and take part in the
discussion. – But: – (a) I gave up coming to the Mor[al] Sc[iences]
Cl[ub] 4 years ago; people then more or less objected to me for
talking too much in their discussions. (b) At the meeting there
will be Broad, who, I believe, objects most strongly to me. On the
other hand (c), if I am to discuss at all it will – in all likelihood –
be the only natural thing for me to say *a good deal*, i.e., to speak for
a considerable time. (d) Even if I speak a good deal I shall probably find that it's hopeless to explain things in such a meeting.

There are therefore the following possibilities: (a) I don't come
to the meeting at all. This is obviously right, unless you *definitely*
want me to come.

(b) I could come but take no part in the discussion. This too is
all right with me, if it is what you want me to do. (c) I come and
speak up whenever you want me to, i.e., whenever you say so.

You may not quite understand my point of view. It is, roughly,
this: If I felt that I had to make a stand against something and that
I could do it with any chance of success I would do it, Broad or
no Broad. But as it is, I feel like someone who's intruding in a tea-
party in which some people don't care to have him. If, on the
other hand, *you* wished me to be there and to speak (in my natural
way, of course) then it would be as if the host wanted me to be at
the tea-party, and in this case I wouldn't care whether any of the
guests objected. – If I don't come to the Mor[al] Sc[iences] Club
some of the members and I could still have a discussion with you
the next day in my room, or just you and I.

I should be glad if you'd write to me a line about this. (Pro-
vided that you don't think that I wrote some sort of polite nonsense or fishing for compliments; etc.) We also could decide what

is the right thing to do just before the meeting, if I could see you for a minute then.

I am pleased that you're reading my M.S. But please don't think it's in any way necessary. You need neither write nor speak a review about it. I know that it isn't as good as it ought to be and, on the other hand, that it might be still worse.

Yours ever

LUDWIG WITTGENSTEIN

paper to the Moral Sciences Club. – The date is presumably 28 November 1935. The paper was "The Limits of Empiricism" which Russell subsequently, on 5 April 1936, read to the Aristotelian Society and which is published in the Society's *Proceedings*.

my M.S. – In all likelihood the so-called Blue Book.

Letters to John Maynard Keynes

1913–1939

K.1   IV. Alleegasse 16
                                              3.1.13.

DEAR KEYNES,

Thanks for your very kind letter. I thought of writing to you just before I got it to tell you that I will not be able to come over to England until or after the beginning of term, there being all sorts of troubles at home. – I excuse your slanging Philosophy as you were just coming from McTaggart and just thinking of me when you did it. I am very glad to hear that you had a good time.

Yours, etc., etc.

LUDWIG WITTGENSTEIN

K.3   Midland Hotel
                                               Manchester
                                               22.6.13.

DEAR KEYNES,

You will perhaps remember that I once told you I wished to give some money to the research fund – or whatever you call it – of King's Coll[ege] in order to let Johnson have it. I was then not decided as to whether I would give a capital sum once for all, or two hundred pounds every year. The latter way has turned out to be by far the most convenient to me. Now I do not know when and to whom to send the money, etc., etc. and as you are the only person who knows about the matter and I do not wish to tell any one else of my acquaintances I cannot help asking your advice about it. You would oblige me very much if you kindly wrote to me about it, unless there is time for your advice till October, when of course I shall be up at Cambridge. My address till the middle of August will be: L.W. *jun.* IV. Alleegasse 16, Austria, Wien.

Yours truly

LUDWIG WITTGENSTEIN

Johnson. – Wittgenstein gave a grant of £200 a year in order to enable W. E. Johnson to cut down his teaching commitments and have more time for research. Cf. R. F. Harrod, *The Life of John Maynard Keynes*, London 1951, p. 162.

K.4

Hochreit
Post Hohenberg
N[ieder]-Ö[sterreich]
16.7.13.

DEAR KEYNES,

   Thanks very much for the trouble you take over my business.–
My reason for not seeing you oftener last term was, that I did not
wish our intercourse to continue without any sign that *you* wished
to continue it.

Yours sincerely

LUDWIG WITTGENSTEIN

K.7   K.u.K. Art. Autodetachement
                                         Feldpost No 186
                                         [Jan 4, 1915]

DEAR KEYNES,

I've got the letter you wrote to me in September. The money will be sent to the registry as soon as the war will be over. Please give my love to Johnson whom I appreciate more and more the longer I haven't seen him.

If you get this please write to me to the above address via the red cross Switzerland.

                                         Yours

                                         L. WITTGENSTEIN

Jan 4, 1915. – Date added by Keynes. Probably the date of receipt, cf. K.8.

K.8   K.u.K. Art. Autodetachement
                                   "Oblt. Gürth"
                                   Feldpost No 186
                                   [1915]

DEAR KEYNES,

Got your letter you wrote January 10th today. I'm very interested to hear that Russell has published a book lately. Could you possibly send it to me and let me pay you after the war? I'd so much like to see it. By the way, you're quite wrong if you think that being a soldier prevents me from thinking about propositions. As a matter of fact I've done a good deal of logical work lately, and hope to do a good deal more soon. – Please give my love to Johnson. The war hasn't altered my private feelings in the least (thank God!!) Or rather: I think I've grown a little milder. I wonder if Russell has been able to make anything out from the notes I gave to Moore last Easter?

                    Yours

                         L. WITTGENSTEIN

Dated by Keynes.
Russell has published a book. – Presumably *Our Knowledge of the External World*, Russell's Lowell Lectures in Boston. See also R.25 and R.29.

K.9   Cassino
                                                          12.6.19.

MY DEAR KEYNES,

Please kindly forward the enclosed letter to Russell's address. I wish I could see him somehow or other, for I am sure he won't be able to understand my book without a very thorough explanation, which can't be written. Have you done any more work on probability? My M-S. contains a few lines about it which, I believe, – solve the essential question.

                              Yours ever

                                    LUDWIG WITTGENSTEIN

enclosed letter. – This is R.36.

K.10   [1923]

DEAR KEYNES!

Thanks so much for sending me the "Reconstruction in Europe". I should have preferred though to have got a line from you personally, saying how you are getting on, etc. Or, are you too busy to write letters? I don't suppose you are. Do you ever see Johnson? If so, please give him my love. I should so much like to hear from him too (*not* about my book but about himself).

So do write to me sometime, if you will condescend to do such a thing.

Yours sincerely
LUDWIG WITTGENSTEIN

Reconstruction in Europe. – Published in the *Manchester Guardian Commercial* for 18 May 1922, but Keynes's reply (printed as an appendix to K.11) seems to show that this letter was sent in 1923.

K.11   Puchberg am Schneeberg
                                                    4.7.24.

MY DEAR KEYNES

Thanks awfully for sending me your books and for your letter
dated 29./3. I have postponed writing to you so long because I
could not make up my mind as to whether to write to you in English or in German. Writing in German makes things easy for me
and difficult for you. On the other hand if I write in English I am
afraid the whole business may become hopeless at MY End already.
Whereas you might find somebody to translate a German letter to
you. If I have said all I've got to say I'll end up in English.

Also: Zuerst möchte ich Ihnen noch einmal für die Bücher und
Ihren lieben Brief danken. Da ich sehr beschäftigt bin und mein
Gehirn für alles Wissenschaftliche ganz unaufnahmsfähig ist, so
habe ich nur in *einem* der Bücher gelesen ("The economic consequences [of the peace]"). Es hat mich sehr interessiert, obwohl ich
von dem Gegenstand natürlich so gut wie nichts verstehe. Sie
schreiben, ob Sie etwas tun könnten, um mir wieder wissenschaft-
liches Arbeiten zu ermöglichen: Nein, in dieser Sache läßt sich
nichts machen; denn ich habe selbst keinen starken inneren Trieb
mehr zu solcher Beschäftigung. Alles was ich wirklich sagen
mußte, habe ich gesagt und damit ist die Quelle vertrocknet. Das
klingt sonderbar, aber es ist so. – Gerne, *sehr* gerne möchte ich
Sie wiedersehen; und ich weiß, daß Sie so gut waren, mir Geld
für einen Aufenthalt in England zuzusichern. Wenn ich aber
denke, daß ich von Ihrer Güte nun wirklich Gebrauch machen
soll, so kommen mir allerlei Bedenken: Was soll ich in England
tun? Soll ich nur kommen um Sie zu sehen und mich auf alle mög-
liche Weise zu zerstreuen? I mean to say shall I just come to be
nice? Now I don't think at all that it isn't worth while being nice –
if only I could be REALLY nice – or having a nice time – if it were
a VERY nice time indeed.

But staying in rooms and having tea with you every other day
or so would not be *nice enough*. But then I should pay for this little
niceness with the great disadvantage of seeing my short holidays
vanish like a phantom without having the least profit – I don't

mean money – or getting any satisfaction from them. Of course staying in Cambridge with you is much nicer than staying in Vienna alone. But in Vienna I can collect my thoughts a little and although they are not worth collecting they are better than mere distraction.

Now it wouldn't seem impossible that I could get more out of you than a cup of tea every other day that's to say that I could really profit from hearing you and talking to you and in this case it would be worth while coming over. But here again there are great difficulties: We haven't met since 11 years. I don't know if you have changed during that time, but I certainly have tremendously. I am sorry to say I am no better than I was, but I am *different*. And therefore if we shall meet you may find that the man who has come to see you isn't really the one you meant to invite. There is no doubt that, even if we *can* make ourselves understood to one another, a chat or two will *not* be sufficient for the purpose, and that the result of our meeting will be disappointment and disgust on your side and disgust and despair on mine. – Had I any definite work to do in England and were it to sweep the streets or to clean anybody's boots I would come over with great pleasure and then nicety could come by itself in course.

There would be a lot more to say about the subject but it's too difficult to express it either in English or in German. So I'd better make an end. I thought when I began to write that I should write this letter altogether in German but, extraordinarily enough, it has proved more natural for me to write to you in broken English than in correct German.

Herzliche Grüße! Yours ever

LUDWIG WITTGENSTEIN

P.S. Please give my love to Johnson if you see him.

(K.11 (part) English Translation)

So: first I should like to thank you once again for the books and for your kind letter. Since I'm very busy and my brain is quite incapable of absorbing anything of a scientific character, I've only read parts of *one* of the books ("The economic consequences of the peace"). It interested me very much, though of course I understand practically nothing about the subject. You ask in your letter whether you could do anything to make it possible for me to return to scientific work. The answer is, No: there's nothing that can be done in that way, because I myself no longer have any strong inner drive towards that sort of activity. Everything that I really *had* to say, I have said, and so the spring has run dry. That sounds queer, but it's how things are. – I'd like – *very much* – to see you again and I know that you've been so kind as to guarantee me money for a stay in England. But when I think that I ought really to avail myself of your kindness, all sorts of misgivings occur to me: what am I to do in England? Shall I come just in order to see you and to amuse myself in every way possible?

This letter is a reply to the following letter by Keynes to Wittgenstein:

46, Gordon Square
Bloomsbury
29 March 1924

MY DEAR WITTGENSTEIN,

A whole year has passed by and I have not replied to your letter. I am ashamed that this should have been so. But it was not for want of thinking about you and of feeling very much that I wanted to renew signs of friendship. The reason was that I wanted to try to understand your book thoroughly before writing to you; yet my mind is now so far from fundamental questions that it is impossible for me to get clear about such matters. I still do not know what to say about your book, except that I feel certain that it is a work of extraordinary importance and genius. Right or wrong, it dominates all fundamental discussions at Cambridge since it was written.

I have sent you in a separate package copies of the various books which I have written since the war. *Probability* is the completion of what I was doing before the war, – I fear you will not like it. Two books on the Peace Treaty, half economic and half political, a book on Monetary Reform (which is what I most think about just now).

I should like immensely to see and talk with you again. Is there a chance that you will pay a visit to England?

Yours truly and affectionately
J. M. KEYNES

You may like to see the enclosed paper about a memorial to Pinsent.

I would do anything in my power which could make it easier for you to do further work.

Wittgenstein's reactions to the suggestion that he should revisit Cambridge are also explained in the following letter from Ramsey to Keynes:

Wien I
Mahlerstrasse 7
Tür 27
Austria
24/3/24

DEAR MAYNARD,

The Puchberg address is right for Wittgenstein. I went to see him yesterday; he was very pleased to have your books, and sends you his love.

He also asked me to write to you about the possibility of his coming to England, because he is afraid he could not express himself adequately in English and you would not understand if he wrote in German. I think he could express himself all right but it would be a great effort and so I said I would try for him. He talked about it to Richard but does not trust Richard to report him faithfully.

He has definitely decided that he wouldn't like to come and stay in Cambridge. July and August are almost the only holiday he gets in the year, and he generally spends them living almost alone in Vienna contemplating. He prefers Vienna to Cambridge unless he has some special reason for going to Cambridge, which could only be to see people. The people in England he wants to see are few; Russell he can no longer talk to, Moore he had some misunderstanding with, and there really only remain you and Hardy, and perhaps Johnson whom he would just like to see, but obviously they wouldn't get on. I shan't be coming back to England till October.

To come to Cambridge and just go out to tea and see people, is, he thinks, not merely not worth while, but positively bad because such intercourse would merely distract him from his contemplation without offering any alternative good; because he feels that he couldn't get into touch with people, even you whom he likes very much, without some effort on both sides and unless he were to see them a good deal.

It comes to this: that, while he would like to stay with you in the country and try to get intimate with you again, he won't come to England just to have a pleasant time, because he would feel it so futile and not enjoy it.

I think he is right about this, but I feel it a pity too, because if he were got away from his surroundings and were not so tired, and had me to stimulate him, he might do some more very good work; and he might conceivably have come to England with that in view. But while he is teaching here I don't think he will do anything, his thinking is so obviously frightfully uphill work as if he were worn out. If I am here during his summer holiday I might try to stimulate him then.

So I'm afraid he won't come to England this year, nor can I advise him to, unless you would like to ask him to stay with you in the country, in which case he would come. (It occurred to him that that was what he would like to do; I didn't suggest it.)

I hope I have made his point of view clear; it is just the opposite of what I imagined. When he wrote that he was afraid of staying with anyone as he might find it difficult and be a bore, I at once thought he might nevertheless like to live alone and see people occasionally. But that he won't do as he thinks he would not understand the people he saw nor they him at once or at all, unless he saw them constantly, as he would staying with them. On the other hand I think he has decided that it would be worth while trying, in spite of the chance of complete failure, if you were to ask him to stay with you.

I'm afraid I think you would find it difficult and exhausting. Though I like him very much I doubt if I could enjoy him for more than a day or two, unless I had my great interest in his work, which provides the mainstay of our conversation.

But I should be pleased if you did get him to come and see you, as it might possibly get him out of this groove.

Yours ever

Frank Ramsey

The letters are reproduced here with the kind permission of Sir Geoffrey Keynes and Mrs Lettice Ramsey. The originals are respectively in the possession of Dr Herman Hänsel of Vienna and of the Library of King's College, Cambridge.

K.12   8.7.25.

DEAR KEYNES,

Some weeks ago I got a letter from a friend of mine in Manchester inviting me to stay with him some time during my holidays. Now I'm not yet quite decided about whether I shall come
or not but I should rather like to, if I could also see *you* during my
stay (about the middle of August). Now please let me know
FRANKLY if you have the slightest wish to see me. If you give me
a negative answer I shan't mind in the least. Please write to me as
soon as possible, as my holidays are rather short and I shall hardly
have time enough to arrange for my journey.

Yours ever

LUDWIG WITTGENSTEIN

My address is: L.W. bei Dr. Hänsel
Wien V., Kriehubergasse 25.

friend of mine in Manchester. – Mr W. Eccles.

K.13   [July or August 1925]

DEAR KEYNES,

Thanks so much for your letter. I will come to London on the 16th at 10h40 in the evening (via Boulogne–Folkestone). Please let me meet you in London as I don't like the idea of travelling about in England alone now. If you will send me some money for the journey I shall be very glad. I'm awfully curious how we are going to get on with one another. It will be exactly like a dream.

                        Yours ever
                                    LUDWIG WITTGENSTEIN

K.14   7.8.25.

DEAR KEYNES,

Thanks very much for your letter and the £10. I will travel by
Dieppe–Newhaven as you suggest and shall arrive at Newhaven
on Tuesday 18th in the morning by the boat which leaves Dieppe
at midnight.

Auf Wiedersehen!

Yours ever

L. WITTGENSTEIN

Wittgenstein spent his time in England in August at Manchester, at
Cambridge, and with Keynes in Sussex. At Cambridge he saw Ramsey
and Johnson, and perhaps other friends too. – Wittgenstein often told
me of his great fondness of W. E. Johnson, to which the letters here
published also testify. Johnson seems patiently to have endured the de-
molishing attacks on his logic which Wittgenstein launched in their
conversations before the war. It reflects the atmosphere of their relations, I think, that Johnson in a note to Keynes of 24 August 1925
wrote: "Tell Wittgenstein that I shall be very pleased to see him once
more; but I must bargain that we don't talk on the foundations of
Logic, as I am no longer equal to having my roots dug up."

K.15   18.10.25.

My dear Keynes,

Thanks so much for your letter! I am still teacher and don't want any money at present. I have decided to remain teacher, as long as I feel that the troubles into which I get that way, may do me any good. If one has toothache it is good to put a hot-water bottle on your face, but it will only be effective, as long as the heat of the bottle gives you some pain. I will chuck the bottle when I find that it no longer gives me the particular kind of pain which will do my character any good. That is, if people here don't turn me out before that time. If I leave off teaching I will probably come to England and look for a job there, because I am convinced that I cannot find anything at all possible in *this* country. In this case I will want your help.

Please remember me to your wife.

Yours ever

Ludwig

Give my love to Johnson, if you see him.

The letter reflects the difficulties of Wittgenstein's life as a school-teacher. After a severe crisis with the people in his environment and the school authorities he resigned his post at the end of April 1926, and did not return to schoolteaching.

K.17   Wien III.
                                                  Parkgasse 18
                                                  [Summer 1927]

MY DEAR KEYNES,

It's ages since you have heard from me. I haven't even thanked
you for your little book about Russia which you sent me about a
year and a half ago. I won't try to explain my long silence: there
were lots of reasons for it. I had a great many troubles one over-
lapping the other and postponed writing until they would be all
over. But now I have interrupted my troubles by a short holiday
and this is the occasion to write to you. I have given up teaching
long ago (about 14 months)* and have taken to architecture. I'm
building a house in Vienna. This gives me heaps of troubles and
I'm not even sure that I'm not going to make a mess of it. However I believe it will be finished about November and then I might
take a trip to England if anybody there should care to see me. I
should VERY much like to see you again and meanwhile to get a
line from you. About your book I forgot to say that I liked it. It
shows that you know that there are more things between heaven
and earth etc.

Please remember me to your wife.

                                                  Yours ever

                                                      LUDWIG

* I couldn't stand the hot bottle any longer.

book about Russia. – *A Short View of Russia* published by the Hogarth
Press in December 1925.

house in Vienna. – This is the house Wittgenstein built for his sister
Mrs M. Stonborough. For a description of the house see Ugo Giaco-
mini, "Un'opera architettonica di Wittgenstein", *Aut Aut, rivista di
filosofia e di cultura,* nr 87, maggio 1965.

My dear Keynes!

I've just finished my house
that has kept me entirely
busy these last few years.
Now however I will have some
holidays & naturally want to
see you again as soon as possible.
The question is, would you want
seeing me. If not, write a line.

(I could come to England in
the first days of December but
not before, as I must first
right part of my anatomy.
Enclosed you will find a few
photos of my house & hope you
won't be to much disgusted
by its simplicity

Yours ever

Rubens

Wien III Kuhdiamangasse 19

vide door.

K.18   Wien III
                                                                 Kundmanngasse 19
                                                                 [1928]

MY DEAR KEYNES,

   I've just finished my house that has kept me entirely busy these
last two years. Now however I will have some holidays and naturally want to see you again as soon as possible. The question is,
would you mind seeing me. If not, write a line. I could come to
England in the first days of December but not before, as I must
first set to rights part of my anatomy. Enclosed you will find a few
photos of my house and hope you won't be too much disgusted
by its simplicity.

                                                         Yours ever

                                                              LUDWIG

Write soon!

   Wien III Kundmanngasse 19. – The address of the house which Wittgenstein built in Vienna.
   parts of my anatomy. – It is not known to me to what sort of bodily
ailment this phrase makes reference.

K.20   Wien III
                                           Kundmanngasse 19
                                           [December 1928]

MY DEAR KEYNES,

  I had to postpone my trip, as my health was not quite strong
enough in the first days of this month. But I am nearly well now
and want to come to England in the beginning of January. Please
write a line letting me know if I can see you then.

                                           Yours ever

                                               LUDWIG

On 3 December 1928 Wittgenstein had sent a telegram to Keynes
saying "Am still unable to travel letter follows Ludwig".

K.21   [May 1929]

DEAR KEYNES,

It is very difficult for me to write this letter to you. Please try to
understand it before you criticize it. (To write it in a foreign language makes it still more difficult.) But I feel I could not come to
you as you wanted me to without beginning to give and perhaps
to ask for long explanations which I am sure you wouldn't like.
When I saw you *last* I was confirmed in a view which had arisen
in me last term already: you then made it very clear to me that you
were tired of my conversation etc. *Now please don't think that I
mind that!* Why shouldn't you be tired of me, I don't believe for a
moment that I can be entertaining or interesting to you. What I
did mind was to hear through your words an undertone of grudge
or annoyance. Perhaps these are not exactly the right words but
it was that sort of thing. I couldn't make out for some time what
could be the cause of it all, until a thought came into my head
which was by an accident proved to be correct. It was this: I
thought probably you think that I cultivate your friendship
amongst other reasons to be able to get some financial assistance
from you if I should be in need (as you imagined I might be some
day). This thought was *very* disagreable to me. I was however
proved right in this way: In the beginning of this term I came to
see you and wanted to return you some money you had lent me.
And in my clumsy way of speaking I prefaced the act of returning
it by saying "Oh, first I want money" meaning "first I want to
settle the money business" or some such phrase. But you naturally
misunderstood me and consequently made a face in which I could
read a whole story. And what followed this, I mean our conversation about the society, showed me what amount of negative feelings you had accumulated in you against me. Now this could
never prevent me from having tea with you; I would be very glad
if I could suppose that your grudge for which I could not see any
good reason had passed away. But the second remark in your letter seems to show me that you don't want to see me as my friend
but as my benefactor. But I don't accept benefactions except from

my friends. (That's why I accepted your help three years ago in Sussex.)

If some day you should want me to have tea with you without talking over my finances I will gladly come. – Please don't answer this letter unless you can write a *short* and *kind* answer. I did not write it to get explanations from you but to inform you about how I think. So if you can't give me a kind answer in three lines, no answer will please me best.

Yours ever

LUDWIG

To this letter Keynes wrote a kind and understanding reply dated 26 May 1929. It was found among Wittgenstein's papers after his death. It is here reprinted with the kind permission of Sir Geoffrey Keynes:

King's College,
Cambridge.
May 26 1929

DEAR LUDWIG,

What a maniac you are! Of course there is not a particle of truth in anything you say about money. It never crossed my mind at the beginning of this term that you wanted anything from me except to cash a cheque or something of that kind. I have never supposed it possible that you could want any money from me except in circumstances in which I should feel it appropriate to give it. When I mentioned your finances in my note the other day, it was because I had heard that you were bothered with heavy unexpected fees and I wanted, if this was so, to examine a possibility which I think I suggested to you when you first came up, namely that some help might conceivably be got out of Trinity. I had considered whether it could be a good thing for me to do anything myself, and had decided on the whole better not.

No – it was not "an undertone of grudge" that made me speak rather crossly when last we met; it was just fatigue or impatience with the difficulty, almost impossibility, when one has a conversation about something affecting you personally, of being successful in conveying true impressions into your mind and keeping false ones out. And then you go away and invent an explanation so remote from anything then in my consciousness that it never occurred to me to guard against it!

The truth is that I alternate between loving and enjoying you and your conversation and having my nerves worn to death by it. It's no new thing! I always have – any time these twenty years. But "grudge" "unkindness" – if only you could look into my heart, you'd see something quite different.

Well, if you can forgive me sufficiently, will you come and dine with me in hall to-night (I shall be away nearly all next week)? – When you can talk or not talk about cash, just as you feel inclined.

Yours ever

JMK

the society. – This could possibly be a reference to the discussion club known as "The Society" or "The Apostles". Cf. below comment to M.4.

three years ago. – Since this presumably refers to Wittgenstein's visit to England in 1925, he ought to have written "four" and not "three".

K.22   [December 1930]

MY DEAR KEYNES,

Thanks so much for your congratulations. Yes, this fellowship
business is very gratifying. Let's hope that my brains will be fer-
tile for some time yet. God knows if they will! – I hope to see you
again some day before the end of this academic year anyhow.

Yours ever

LUDWIG

fellowship. – Refers to Wittgenstein's appointment to a Fellowship at
Trinity College in December 1930. Cf. above, Introduction, p. 3.

K.25   Sunday 30.6.[35.]

MY DEAR KEYNES,

I'm sorry I must trouble you with my affairs again. There are two things I want to ask you:

(a) I thought the other day when we talked in your room you were not disinclined to give me some sort of introduction to Maiski the Ambassador. I then said I thought he would not be the man who would give me the advice I wanted. But I've been told since that *if* he were inclined to give me a letter of introduction to some officials in Russia it would help me a lot. Therefore my first question is, would you be willing to give me an introduction to Maiski so as to make it possible for me to have a conversation with him, as the result of which he *might* give me an introduction?

(b) I have now more or less decided to go to Russia as a Tourist in September and see whether it is possible for me to get a suitable job there. If I find (which, I'm afraid is quite likely) that I can't find such a job, or get permission to work in Russia, then I should want to return to England and if possible study Medicine. Now when you told me that you would finance me during my medical training you did not know, I think, that I wanted to go to Russia and that I would try to get permission to practise medicine in Russia. I know that you are not in favour of my going there (and I think I understand you). Therefore I must ask you whether, under these circumstances, you would still be prepared to help me. I don't like to ask you this question, not because I risk a "No", but because I hate asking any questions about this matter. If you reply please just write on a P.C.:

(a) No or (a) Yes, etc.

(b) No, etc.

as the case may be. I shall not think it the least unkind of you if you answer both *a* and *b* negatively.

I left your room the other day with a sad feeling. It is only too natural that you shouldn't entirely understand what makes me do what I am doing, nor how hard it is for me.

Yours ever

LUDWIG

trouble you with my affairs again. – This perhaps refers to the fact that Wittgenstein in the spring of 1935 had been discussing with Keynes his plans of publishing the book on which he was then working. Keynes mentions this in a letter to Moore of 6 March 1935. Keynes expressed his willingness to contribute to the printing costs, should the publication plans meet with financial difficulties. Wittgenstein seems to have wanted his work published under the auspices of the British Academy.

Maiski. – Ivan Mikhailovitch Maisky, b. 1884, Ambassador of USSR to Great Britain 1932–1943.

K.26   Saturday 6.7.35.

My dear Keynes,

   Thanks for your letter. To thank you for your answer to point
(a) wouldn't be the right thing, for no word of thanks would be
really adequate. – As to (b) I can't see Vinogradoff because he has
left for Moscow. He told me he was going to leave on the Saturday after my conversation with him. In this conversation he
wasn't at all very helpful i.e. not as helpful even as *he* might have
been. I'm sure however he didn't show this when you asked him
about me in the presence of Maisky. Vinogradoff was *exceedingly
careful* in our conversation and I'm sure he has to be. He of course
knew as well as anyone that recommendations might help me but
it was quite clear that he wasn't going to help me to get any, at
least none that might carry real weight. – Now what I wanted
with Maisky was this: I wanted to see him and have a conversation with him. I know that there is VERY little chance that I or my
case could make a good impression on him. But I think there is an
off chance of this happening. There is further a small chance of his
knowing some official at Leningrad or Moscow to whom he might
introduce me. I want to speak to officials at two institutions; one
is the "Institute of the north" in Leningrad, the other the "Institute of national Minorities" in Moscow. These Institutes, as I am
told, deal with people who want to go to the 'colonies' the newly
colonized parts at the periphery of the U.S.S.R. I want to get information and possibly help from people in these Institutes. I
thought that Maisky might recommend me to someone there. I
imagine that such a recommendation or introduction could be of
two kinds. It may either be purely official; in which case it could
only say "would so and so be so kind to *see* me and listen to my
questions". For it is clear to me that Maisky could not do anything else qua Ambassador. Or it might be an unofficial recommendation to someone he knows well and this he would only give
me if I made a good impression on him, which – *I know* – is very
unlikely. If what I think is sound – and God knows whether it is –
then it might be useful for me to get an introduction from you to

Maisky. In this introduction I don't want you to *ask* him to give me introductions, but only to allow me to have a conversation with him in order to get some information or advice. If he grants me an interview I will myself ask him whether he could give me an introduction to someone in Russia: you would have to say in your introduction that I am your personal friend and that you are sure that I am in no way politically dangerous (that is, if this *is* your opinion). – If you feel, either that such an introduction and consequent conversation could do me no good or if you feel uncomfortable about giving me such an introduction for any other reasons, whatever they may be, I will feel PERFECTLY satisfied with your not giving me an introduction.

I am sure that you partly understand my reasons for wanting to go to Russia and I admit that they are partly bad and even childish reasons but it is true also that behind all that there are deep and even good reasons.

Yours ever

LUDWIG

To this Keynes replied (10.7.) as follows:

DEAR LUDWIG,

I enclose a letter of introduction to Maisky. I suggest that you might send this to him with a covering note asking if he could manage to spare the time to give you an interview.

I gathered from Vinogradoff that the difficulty would be that you have to receive an invitation from some Soviet organisation. If you were a qualified technician of any description of a sort likely to be useful to them, that might not be difficult. But, without some such qualification, which might very well be a medical qualification, it would be difficult.

Yours ever

JMK

Keynes's letter of introduction to Maisky:

DEAR MONSIEUR MAISKY,

May I venture to introduce to you Dr Ludwig Wittgenstein, a Fellow of Trinity College, Cambridge, who is anxious to find means of obtaining permission to live more or less permanently in Russia.

Dr Wittgenstein, who is a distinguished philosopher, is a very old and intimate friend of mine, and I should be extremely grateful for anything you could do for him. I must leave it to him to tell you his reasons for wanting to go to Russia. He is not a member of the Communist Party, but has strong sympathies with the way of life which he believes the new régime in Russia stands for.

I may mention that Dr Wittgenstein is an Austrian subject, though he has had long periods of residence in Cambridge both before and since the war. He has already had an interview with Mr Vinogradoff, who gave him some preliminary advice, but I gather that Mr Vinogradoff is no longer in England.

K.27   Friday
                                                   [July 1935]

DEAR KEYNES,

   This is only to thank you for your introduction and to tell you
that my interview with Maisky went off all right. He was definitely
nice and in the end promised to send me some addresses of people
in Russia of whom I might get useful information. He did not seem
to think that it was utterly hopeless for me to try to get permission to settle in Russia though he too didn't think it was likely.

                                                   Yours ever

                                                   LUDWIG

   Wittgenstein visited Russia early in the autumn of 1935. After his return to Cambridge from his year in Norway, 1936–1937, he still had
plans to go to Russia. See Paul Engelmann, *Letters from Ludwig Wittgenstein*, p. 58.

K.28   81, East Rd
                                                Cambridge
                                                1.2.39.

DEAR KEYNES,

I went round to King's College last night with the M.S. but was told that you had gone to London; so I took it back again and shall keep it till Friday unless you want it before then. I want to use the two days to look a little through the translation and perhaps correct some of the worst mistakes. I haven't yet had time to do this (queer as this may sound). My translator did about half of the first volume and then had to leave for America where his father died some weeks ago. I'll also give you the German text – in case it's any use to you. Not that I think that it's worth your while looking at it, or at the translation; but as you wish to see it of course you'll get it. (Moore has read most of the German text and might possibly be able to give some information about it.) I'm afraid there's *only one* copy of the English in existence and only one *corrected* copy of the German; you'll get these two copies.

Thanks ever so much for taking all this trouble (in what I believe to be a lost cause).

Yours ever

LUDWIG

M.S. – A translation into English of the beginning of the then existing version of the *Investigations*.

lost cause. – Wittgenstein had applied for the professorship of philosophy which was to become vacant after Moore's retirement. Keynes was one of the Electors to the Chair.

K.29   81, East Rd
                                                                      Cambridge
                                                                      3.2.39.

MY DEAR KEYNES,

When yesterday I began to look through the English translation of my book I saw that it was a good deal worse than I had expected, so correcting it seemed almost hopeless. But I went through it nevertheless, as far as I could get in these two days, and corrected it almost word for word, as you will see when you look at the English M.S. I couldn't do more than about 20 pages in this way. If you can read a little German I should try to read the German text. The whole thing seems even more of a farce now than it did a few days ago.

                              Good wishes!
                                       Yours ever
                                              LUDWIG

K.30   81, East Rd
                                                   Cambridge
                                                   8.2.39.

DEAR KEYNES,

Thanks for your kind notes. Yes, the translation is pretty awful, and yet the man who did it is an *excellent* man. Only he's not a born translator, and nothing's more difficult to translate than colloquial (non-technical) prose.

Yours ever

LUDWIG

K.31

81, East Rd
Cambridge
11.2.39.

MY DEAR KEYNES,

Thanks for the telegram, and thanks for all the trouble you've gone to. I hope to God that you haven't made a mistake. I know, it's up to me to prove that you haven't. Well, I *hope* I'll be a decent prof.

Thanks again
Yours ever
LUDWIG

telegram. – Evidently a telegram of congratulation on the occasion of Wittgenstein's election to the professorship on 11 February 1939.

Letters to George Edward Moore

1913–1948

M.2   c/o H. Draegni
Skjolden, Sogn, Norway
19.11.13.

DEAR MOORE,

Many thanks for your P.C. I am very sorry that you feel so miserable at times about your work. I think, the cause of it is, that you don't regularly discuss your stuff with anybody who is not yet stale and is *really* interested in the subject. And I believe that at present there is no such person up at Cambridge. Even Russell – who is of course most extraordinarily fresh for his age – is no more pliable enough for *this* purpose. Don't you think it would be a good thing if we had regular discussions when you come to me at Easter? Not – of course – that I am any good at the subject! But I am not yet stale and care for it very much. I can't help thinking that this would make you lose your feeling of sterility. I think you ought to think about your problems with the view to discussing them with me at Easter. Now don't you think that I am arrogant in saying this! I don't for a moment believe that I could get as clear about your questions as you can, but – as I said before – I am not yet wasted and am very interested in the stuff. *Do* think this over. – Let me hear from you soon.

Yours most, etc.

L. WITTGENSTEIN

M.3   [Postcard stamped at Sogn 30.1.14.]

About 2 months ago I wrote to you asking you to write to me
about Johnson's lecture, and I haven't got an answer yet. Isn't
that a shame? Also I should like to know how you are and when
the Easter vac's begin. Have you ever thought about the nature
of a tautology? That's what I am now bothered with.

Now *do* write to me soon and much!

Yours, etc., etc.

LUDWIG WITTGENSTEIN

P.S. I am now learning to ski and find it great fun.

Johnson's lecture. – Since there is no mention of a lecture by Johnson
in M.2 there evidently existed a letter from Wittgenstein to Moore
written after 19 November 1913 which is now lost.

M.4   Skjolden
                                                        18.2.14.

DEAR MOORE,

Thanks so much for your letter. I'm sorry I caused you horrid troubles. I didn't really expect such a long account of the meeting. But all you wrote to me interested me enormously because I think I know exactly what Johnson was at. It – of course – all turns on the question as to the nature of deduction. And – I think – the clue to it all lies in the fact that $\varphi x \supset_x \psi x$ only then expresses the deductive relation when this prop[osition] is the generalization of a tautology.

You must come as soon as Term ends and I shall meet you in Bergen. I am looking forward to your coming more than I can say! I am bothered to death with Logik and other things. But I hope I shan't die before you come for in that case we couldn't discuss *much*.

                                                        Yours, etc.

                                                        L.W.

P.S. Boats run from Newcastle to Bergen 3 times a week. I shall expect you in Bergen about the 20th of March. What has happened with young Sedgwick whom Hardy [tried] to run? Has he become a member of the Society?

Logik. – See comment on *M*.8 below.

Sedgwick. – The reference is presumably to R. R. Sedgwick, b. 1894, then an undergraduate and later a fellow of Trinity College.

Hardy. – G. H. Hardy, the mathematician.

the Society. – The semi-secret, ancient discussion club at Cambridge also known as "The Apostles". Russell, Moore, and Keynes were members of the Society. Russell had in 1912 proposed Wittgenstein for membership. For an account of the activities of the Society in the years before the first world war see Russell's *Autobiography* I, pp. 68–70 and *passim*.

M.6   [Skjolden, Sogn, Norway]
                               [March 1914]

DEAR MOORE,

Why on earth won't you do your paper *here*? You shall have *a sittingroom* with a splendid view ALL BY YOURSELF and I shall leave you alone as much as you like (*in fact the whole day, if necessary*). On the other hand we *could* see one another whenever both of us should like to. And we *could* even talk over your business (which *might* be fun). Or do you want *so* many books? You see – I've PLENTY to do myself, so I shan't disturb you a bit. *Do* take the Boat that leaves Newcastle on the 17th arriving in Bergen on the 19th and do your work here (I might even have a good influence upon it by preventing too many repetitions). I *think*, now, that Logic must be very nearly done if it is not already. – So, DO think over what I've said!!

                               Yours, etc., etc.

                               L.W.

P.S. Oh – *Do* buy the "Schicksalslied" by Brahms in an arrangement for 4 hands and bring it with you. And, please, send a telegram if you come on the 19th. I *hope* you will.

On 10 March 1914 Wittgenstein had cabled to Moore: "Do your paper here you shall get your own sittingroom writing Wittgenstein."

Logic. – This is perhaps a reference to the same thing referred to as 'Logik' in *M.*4. See comment on *M.*8 below.

M.7   Skjolden
                                                         5.3.14.

DEAR MOORE,

Only a few lines because I'm just now in the right mood. First of all: *write* soon when exactly you're going to come to Bergen. Secondly: *come* soon. Thirdly: I've got out LOTS of new logical stuff. (I don't dare to say more.) Fourthly: If you see Johnson please give him my kindest regards. Fifthly: if you see Muscio *please* tell him that he's a *beast* (he'll know why). Sixthly: once more – come soon. That's all.

                                                    Yours, etc., etc.

                                                         L.W.

Muscio. – Bernard Muscio (1887–1928), University Demonstrator in Experimental Psychology at Cambridge, later Professor of Philosophy, University of Sydney.

M.8   May 7, '14

DEAR MOORE,

Your letter annoyed me. *When I wrote Logik I didn't consult the Regulations*, and therefore I think it would only be fair if you gave me my degree without consulting them so much either! As to a Preface and Notes; I think my examiners will easily see how much I have cribbed from Bosanquet. – If I'm not worth your making an exception for me *even in some* STUPID *details* then I may as well go to Hell directly; and if I *am* worth it and you don't do it then – by God – *you* might go there.

The whole business is too stupid and too beastly to go on writing about it so –

                                                               L.W.

my degree. – The letter seems to indicate that Wittgenstein had submitted an essay for the Bachelor of Arts degree, which an Advanced Student (p. 1) would normally be expected to take. Nothing definite is known about this. According to the regulations for Advanced Students, such a dissertation was expected to contain a *preface* and *notes* in which the student had to state the sources on which he had relied and "the extent to which he had availed himself of the work of others". There is a diary entry by Moore which would indicate that Moore had shown the stuff to W. M. Fletcher, tutor at Trinity College (see above, p. 1), and been told that it could not possibly pass for a dissertation. Thereupon he had written to Wittgenstein about this, provoking his angry and probably unjustified reaction. It is of some interest to note that Wittgenstein is referring to the writing under the German title *Logik*. This may be taken as an indication that the proposed dissertation was written in German. How, if at all, it was related to the "Notes on Logic" we do not know. It can hardly, however, be identified with the German *Urtext* of the Notes (see above, comment on R.18, p. 294). For, considering *M.4* and *M.6*, it seems that Wittgenstein was still working on the "dissertation" in February and March 1914.

Bosanquet. – Evidently a reference, meant to be ironic, to the philosopher Bernard Bosanquet and to his work *Logic*.

M.9   Wien XVII
                                   Neuwaldeggerstraße 38
                                   July 3rd, '14

DEAR MOORE,

Upon clearing up some papers before leaving Skjolden I popped upon your letter which had made me so wild. And upon reading it over again I found that I had probably no sufficient reason to write to you as I did. (Not that I like your letter a bit *now*.) But at any rate my wrath has cooled down and I'd rather be friends with you again than otherwise. I consider I have strained myself enough now for I would *not* have written this to many people and if you don't answer this I shan't write to you again.

Yours, etc., etc.

L.W.

Neuwaldeggerstraße. – The address of a big house which the Wittgenstein family had on the outskirts of Vienna.

The date of the letter is probably that of reception by Moore.

Moore had every reason to be offended by Wittgenstein's previous letter (M.8). He did not reply to M.8 or to M.9. In an autobiographical annotation Moore says that after the "violent letter of abuse" (M.8) he had no contact with Wittgenstein until Wittgenstein's return to Cambridge in January 1929. Cf. above, Introduction, p. 4.

M.11   [Cambridge]
                                              Saturday
                                              [15 June 1929]

DEAR MOORE,

   Mr Butler wrote to me on Thursday to see him about the research-grant and to explain what exactly it was I wanted, and what were my plans for the future. – I did my best to explain it but don't feel sure that I have succeeded in making myself clear. I therefore, in this letter, want to state again as clearly as I can my position, to guard against all possibilities of misinterpretation.

   I am in the middle of a bit of research work which I don't want to break off as it seems to me hopeful. I possess all in all about 100 £ which will carry me through the vacations and perhaps another month or two; but I mustn't use up all I've got, to leave some reserve for the time of looking round for a job. – I therefore ask the College to grant me say 50 £ which would enable me to go on with my philosophical work till, at least, Xmas. If it should turn out, that in this time I have been able to produce good work – as judged by anybody the College would consider an expert in the matter – and *if*, further, I should feel capable of continuing my work with success, *then* I propose to ask the College again for some sort of subvention.

   Now Mr Butler asked me, how long, I thought, this might go on. – I can't answer this question, because I don't know, how long I will be able to produce good work. (For all I know – though I don't think it's likely – I may cease tomorrow.) But, I think, this question rests on a misunderstanding of what I really want. Let me explain this: Supposing I was run over by a bus to-day and then were to see my tutor and say: "I'm now a cripple for lifetime, couldn't the College give me some money to support me." Then it would be right to ask the question: "And how long do you propose this to go on, and when will you be self-support-ing?" But this is *not* my case. I propose to do work, and I have a vague idea, that the College in some cases encourages such work by means of research grants, fellowships, etc. That's to say, I turn out some sort of goods and *if* the College has any use for these goods, I would like the College to enable me to produce them, as long as it *has* use for them, and as long as I *can* produce them. – If, on the other hand, the College has no use for them, that puts an end to the question.

Yours ever

LUDWIG WITTGENSTEIN

The date of the letter is by Moore.

Mr Butler. – Sir James Butler, b. 1889, then Tutor in Trinity College, later Regius Professor of Modern History at Cambridge.

On 19 June 1929 the Council of Trinity College authorised a grant of £100 to be made to Wittgenstein to enable him to carry on his research at Cambridge. £50 was to be paid at Midsummer and £50 at Michaelmas.

Anybody who knew Wittgenstein will find this letter and the next extremely characteristic of their author.

M.12   Tuesday
                                              [18 June 1929]
DEAR MOORE,

   This is a P.S. to my last letter. I met Mr Butler in the street today and he asked me 1.) whether you knew all about my financial
position (I said, you did) 2.) Whether I had no other sources of
getting money (I said, no) 3.) Whether I had not got relations who
could help me (I said, I had and had told you so). Now as it somehow appears as if I tried to conceal something, will you please accept my written declaration that: not only I have a number of
wealthy relations, but also that they would give me money if I
asked them to. BUT THAT I WILL NOT ASK THEM FOR A PENNY. (Unless – of course – they owed me money.) Also I will add, that this
is not a mere caprice of mine.

                              Yours ever
                                    LUDWIG WITTGENSTEIN

Dated by Moore.

M.13   [March or April 1930]

DEAR MOORE,

I am in Vienna now, doing the most loathsome work of dictating a synopsis from my manuscripts. It is a terrible bit of work and I feel wretched doing it. I saw Russell the other day at Petersfield and, against my original intention, started to explain to him Philosophy. Of course we couldn't get very far in two days but he seemed to understand a *little* bit of it. My plan is to go and see him in Cornwall on the 22ⁿᵈ or 23ʳᵈ of April and to give him the synopsis and a few explanations. Now my lectures begin on Monday the 28ᵗʰ and I want to know if it is all right if I come to Cambridge not before the 26ᵗʰ. Please write to me about this as soon as possible as I have to make my plans accordingly. I am kindhearted therefore I wish you a good vacation although I haven't a good one myself.

Yours ever
LUDWIG WITTGENSTEIN

Address:
L.W. bei Dr Wollheim
IV. Prinz Eugen Str. 18
Austria Wien

synopsis. – Refers to the typescript of *Philosophische Bemerkungen* mentioned in R.55.

Petersfield. – The Beacon Hill School which Russell and Dora Black had founded in 1927 was near the town of Petersfield in Hampshire. Wittgenstein had come to see Russell there in the middle of March before going, in the beginning of April, to Austria. After his return he went to see Russell who was then on a holiday in Cornwall.

See also R.55 and comments.

M.14   18.6.30.

DEAR MOORE,

Thanks so much for the good news. I'm very grateful to the
Council for its munificence.

I'm glad to hear you are enjoying your holidays. I don't yet enjoy mine, for I haven't yet been able to do any proper work,
partly, I believe, due to the oppressive heat we've had here during
the last week or so, and partly because my brain simply won't
work. I hope to God this state won't last long. It is very depress-
ing when all the lights are put out as if there had *never* been any
burning. However, I dare say it'll pass over. – Would you be so
very kind and take the Midsummer £50 for me and send them on
to my Address? If it's not too much trouble for you I should be
very much obliged if you would.

I hope your vacation will continue satisfactorily and that mine
will soon be all right too. I'd be very glad if you would let me hear
from you again some time how you're getting on, etc.

Yours ever

LUDWIG WITTGENSTEIN

grateful to the Council. – On the basis of reports from Russell and J. E.
Littlewood the Council of Trinity College had granted Wittgenstein
another £100 to enable him to continue his research at Cambridge. See
comments to R.55.

Address. – Refers evidently to Wittgenstein's address during the
Long Vacation, which he spent in Austria.

M.15   26.7.
                                                      [1930?]

DEAR MOORE,

This is to tell you that I have only just now begun to do any proper work at all. Until about a week ago I hardly did any and what work I did wasn't any good. I can't imagine what could have been the matter with me, but I felt both extremely excitable and incapable of sticking to any thought. It may have been some sort of tiredness or the climate, for we had a terrible hot South wind blowing almost all the time which has a bad effect on many people. However I hope it's over now, I'm in the country again since about 10 days, in the same place where I was last year and I'm quite alone at present. – I have received the £50 from Trinity. My life now is very economical, in fact as long as I'm here there is no possibility of spending any money. I hope you're getting on all right.

Yours ever

LUDWIG WITTGENSTEIN

The annotation about the year with the question mark is by Moore. There is every reason to believe that it is correct.

same place. – On the Hochreit. Cf. also M.16.

M.16   [1930]

DEAR MOORE,

Thanks for your letter. I'm sorry you have such trouble at home. These illnesses are a bl[oody] nuisance. – My work is getting on moderately well but not more than that, I hardly ever feel quite alive. The weather is tolerable though rather changeable. Desmond Lee, whom you know, came to Austria and stayed with my people near where I live for a few days. We talked about you and wondered whether you'd like the place. And I almost think you would. I'm going to stay here as long as possible to get something done.

Yours ever

L. WITTGENSTEIN

Lee. – Sir Desmond Lee, b. 1908, then an undergraduate and student of classics at Corpus Christi College, Cambridge. Lee stayed with Wittgenstein's family on the Hochreit in 1930. Wittgenstein himself was living in a gamekeeper's cottage on the estate.

M.17   23.8.31.

DEAR MOORE,

Thanks for your letter. I can quite imagine that you don't admire Weininger very much, what with that beastly translation and the fact that W. must feel very foreign to you. It is true that he is fantastic but he is *great* and fantastic. It isn't necessary or rather not possible to agree with him but the greatness lies in that with which we disagree. It is his enormous mistake which is great. I.e. roughly speaking if you just add a "~" to the whole book it says an important truth. However we better talk about it when I come back. – I've had a very busy time since I left Cambridge and have done a fair amount of work. Now I want you to do me a favour: I don't intend to give any formal lectures this term as I think I must reserve all my strength for my own work. I will however have *private* (unpaid) discussions with students if there are any who want them. That's to say I don't want to be mentioned in the lecture list this term but at the same time Braithwaite could tell his students (and you can tell yours) that if any of them wish to have conversations with me I will arrange times with them. Please write a line to Braithwaite to explain this before the beginning of September. During the first month of the vac we had terribly hot weather and now it's abominably cold and rainy. I'm sorry to hear that the weather in England depresses you, I'm not as fit as I ought to be either.

Yours ever

LUDWIG WITTGENSTEIN

Weininger. – Otto Weininger (1880–1903) was an author whom Wittgenstein greatly admired. The book here referred to is probably the English translation of Weininger's most famous work, *Geschlecht und Charakter* (*Sex and Character*).

private discussions. – Throughout the academic year 1931–1932 Wittgenstein held (unpaid) conversation classes but did not give formal lectures.

M.19   Saturday
                                                                    [1933]

DEAR MOORE,

   Enclosed please find the proof of my letter to Mind. I have
made no corrections. Please read it through and see whether there
is anything to be altered. I wonder whether the comma after
"*Now*" in line 8 is necessary and that after "*print*". If not I'd
rather leave them out. Also the comma after "*think*" three lines
below seems to me not necessary.

                                  Yours ever

                                        LUDWIG WITTGENSTEIN

   letter to Mind. – The letter is dated Cambridge, 27th May 1933 and
was published in the July issue of *Mind* for that year. Moore was then
Editor of *Mind*. In the letter Wittgenstein disclaimed responsibility for
views and thoughts attributed to him in a recent publication. The suggested alterations were made in the printed text.

M.20   Monday
                                                    [October 1933]
DEAR MOORE,

I think I ought to let you know that I am not going to come to
tea with you on Tuesdays. I ought to have written this to you 2
or 3 weeks ago and in fact I wrote a letter to you about a fortnight
ago but destroyed it again. Then I left Cambridge for a week and
postponed writing to you and forgot about it. Please forgive me
my negligence.

I also want you to know that my reason for not coming is a lack
of friendliness which you showed on two occasions, the second
when we last met. (You weren't *un*friendly.) Your behaviour then
made me think that the way we used to meet wasn't quite the right
expression of our actual relation. I know this is expressed very
badly but you'll understand me.

If you will allow me occasionally to turn up at your at home
after tea I'll do so.

                              Yours

                                    LUDWIG WITTGENSTEIN

Dated by Moore.
at home. – Moore's "at homes" were occasions on which philosophical topics were taken up for discussion.

M.21   Saturday
                                                  [December 1933 ?]

DEAR MOORE,

This is the estimate. None of my lectures is over 1200 words and if we have them printed on foolscap they will each cost 4/6 that's to say 20 copies will cost that. Now I don't know exactly how many lectures there will be as possibly I might decide to dictate three times a week next term instead of only twice as I did this term. I dictated only 10 times this term so on the whole there will be about 52 lectures this academic year at the most, and these will cost between 11 and 12 pounds. If we only print 15 copies of each lecture, and there is no earthly reason why we should have more, they'll cost 10% less, i.e. *about £10.*

                              Yours

                                        LUDWIG WITTGENSTEIN

I wish you and Mrs Moore a happy Christmas and New Year.

The lectures are those which Wittgenstein dictated to his class in the academic year 1933–1934 and of which a small number of copies were mimeographed and circulated. They have become known under the name The Blue Book. (See above comments on R.56 and R.57.)

M.22   Monday
                                        [September 1934]

DEAR MOORE,

Thanks for your letter. I wish to God you would attend my classes! It would give me ever so much more of a chance to make things clear, to you *and* to others. Would you come if I promised to provide a very comfortable chair and tobacco and pipecleaners? I came up a week ago and am leaving for Ireland on Friday and shall be back again on October 1st. I shall try to see you on Tuesday Oct. 2nd, i.e. I'll call and see if you are in. – I'm extremely sorry about Priestley!

                          Yours

                               LUDWIG WITTGENSTEIN

Dated by Moore.
classes. – Moore seems not to have attended Wittgenstein's classes in 1934–1935.
Priestley. – The reference is to a close friend of Wittgenstein's, Sir Raymond Edward Priestley, b. 1886, then Secretary General to the Faculties, later Principal and Vice-Chancellor of the University of Birmingham. Priestley was to leave Cambridge and become Vice-Chancellor of Melbourne University at the end of the Michaelmas Term 1934.

M.26   Thursday
                                      [19 March 1936]

DEAR MOORE,

The Thomsons want you and me to come to them tomorrow at teatime. (They live: Lavender Cottage, Storey's Way off Huntingdon Rd.) Now I don't feel very well, I may have a slight 'flu or something, so I probably shan't be able to come. But they should like to see you without me, and possibly you might play some piano duets with Mrs Thomson. So would you go there, say at 4.15 or if you can't, write them a note?

                     Yours

                                      LUDWIG WITTGENSTEIN

I wish I could be there and hear you play!

Dated by Moore.

The Thomsons. – The reference is to Wittgenstein's friend George Thomson, b. 1903, Fellow of King's College, later Professor of Greek in the University of Birmingham, and to his wife, née Stuart.

M.28   Tuesday
                                     [2 June 1936]

DEAR MOORE,

I am having a social gathering of my students in my room, on
Friday at 4.30. Would you mind coming? If I don't hear from you
I shall expect you.

                    Yours

                            LUDWIG WITTGENSTEIN

   Dated by Moore.
   After the end of the academic year 1935–1936 Wittgenstein's fellowship at Trinity expired. In the summer he settled down in his hut in
Norway. He was first working on a German version of the so-called
Brown Book which he had dictated to Alice Ambrose and Francis
Skinner in 1934–1935. He soon abandoned this and made a fresh start
which resulted in a first version of the *Philosophical Investigations*. Wittgenstein's stay in Norway lasted for nine months, interrupted only by
a visit to Vienna and England round New Year 1937. See M.31.

M.29   Wednesday
                                                  [October 1936]

DEAR MOORE,

I was very glad to get your letter. My house is not built on the
site you mean. This map will show you where it is and why I can't

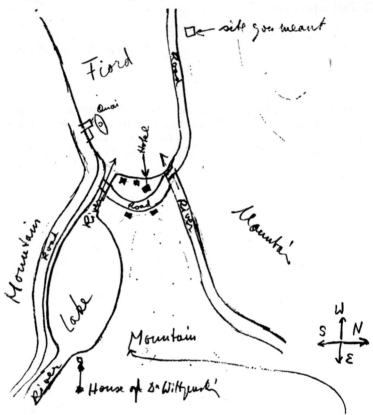

get into the village without rowing; for the Mountain is much too
steep for anyone to walk on it along the lake. I do believe that it
was the right thing for me to come here thank God. I can't
imagine that I could have worked anywhere as I do here. It's the
quiet and, perhaps, the *wonderful* scenery; I mean, its quiet serious-
ness.

I am sorry to hear that your work hasn't been going well, or satisfactorily. I'm sure somehow that you're doing good work, and at the same time I think I can understand why you don't get "anything finally written". That, I think, shows that what you're doing is right. I don't mean that it would be wrong however if you got anything finally written and in fact I hope you *will*. Rhees' case is, of course, quite different, but here too I can't help feeling that it's not bad, *in fact that it's good that he found himself unable to write anything*. Please, if you see him, remember me to him and tell him that I was glad to hear that he could not get anything written. That's a *good* sign. One can't drink wine while it ferments, but that it's fermenting shows that it isn't dish-water. You see, I still make beautiful similes. – Tell Rhees that I'm not glad because I'm malicious.

We have had the most wonderful weather for the last 4 weeks, though it's already getting cold. The waterfalls are entirely frozen and it's about − 3° C. at nights. But I don't suffer from the cold as I would in England, for it's dry.

Remember me to Mrs Moore and to Hardy and Littlewood if you should see them.

Yours

LUDWIG WITTGENSTEIN

Dated by Moore.
The letter from Moore to which Wittgenstein's letter is a reply has been preserved. It is dated Cambridge, September 30, 1936. In his letter Moore recalls the days when he visited Wittgenstein in Norway and asks about the place of Wittgenstein's hut. The hut had not yet been built when Moore was in Norway in 1914. (Cf. R.28.) Moore's letter begins: "I was glad to hear from you, and glad that your work has been going pretty well." The letter from Wittgenstein to which Moore was replying seems to be lost.

M.30   Wednesday
                                          [November 1936]

DEAR MOORE

Enclosed please find the photos. I don't know whether they are
any d. . . . good, but anyhow they're easily as good as I am. One –
in the Botanical garden – was taken in Dublin by Drury, the other
two by Pattisson in France. The one on which I look like an old
prophet was taken when I was rather ill. The one with the bridge
in the background was taken while I was taking a photo myself.
If you don't like them throw them away and I'll send you better
ones when there will be some. I enclose a p[ost] c[ard] which
shows exactly where my hut stands though it doesn't show the
hut, which was built after the picture was taken. The scaffolding
you see in the foreground does no longer exist and, I think, only
bits of it existed when you saw it before the war.

                              Yours

                                   LUDWIG WITTGENSTEIN

Dated by Moore.
  Drury. – Dr Maurice O'Connor Drury, a close friend of Wittgenstein's at Cambridge and later in Dublin.
  Pattisson. – Gilbert Pattisson also became a close friend of Wittgenstein's while an undergraduate at Cambridge and Wittgenstein always
called on him on his way through London in the 30's. The two men
spent a short holiday in France in July 1936.

M.31   Thursday
                                                         20 Nov. [1936]
DEAR MOORE,

I was glad to get your letter. My work isn't going badly. I don't
know if I wrote to you that when I came here I began to translate
into and rewrite in German the stuff I had dictated to Skinner and
Miss Ambrose. When about a fortnight ago, I read through what
I had done so far I found it all, or nearly all, boring and artificial.
For having the English version before me had cramped my thinking. I therefore decided to start all over again and not to let my
thoughts be guided by anything but themselves. – I found it
difficult the first day or two but then it became easy. And so I'm
writing now a new version and I hope I'm not wrong in saying
that it's somewhat better than the last. – Besides this all sorts of
things have been happening inside me (I mean in my mind). I
won't write about them now, but when I come to Cambridge, as I
intend to do for a few days about New Year, I hope to God I shall
be able to talk to you about them; and I shall then want your advice and your help in some very difficult and serious matters. –

I was very glad to hear that Skinner came to the Mor[al]
Sc[iences] Club and that he spoke. I wish it were possible for you
to see him once in a while! It would do him masses of good. For
he *needs* someone he can talk to decently and seriously!

If ever you see Ryle or write to him give him my love. I can
quite imagine that he didn't read a good paper and also that he
was nice and decent and agreeable in the discussion.

I intend to leave here for Vienna about Dec. 8th and to come to
Cambridge about the 30th Dec. and to stay *about* a week.

                           Best wishes!

                                        LUDWIG WITTGENSTEIN

stuff I had dictated. – The so called Brown Book. Cf. comments to
M.28 above. Wittgenstein's German version of part of this (with an in-
dependent translation of the rest of the book) has now been published
as *Eine philosophische Betrachtung* in L. Wittgenstein *Schriften 5* (Suhrkamp, Frankfurt, 1970).

new version. – This is a first version of the *Investigations* up to section 189. The manuscript which was written in a big bound notebook Wittgenstein gave as a Christmas gift to his sister, Mrs Stonborough. The notebook was in Mrs Stonborough's house at Gmunden in 1952, but is now apparently lost.

talk to you. – When Wittgenstein visited Vienna and England round New Year 1937 he talked to several of his friends about personal matters and his inner struggles. He referred to these talks as "confessions". Cf. Paul Engelmann, *Letters from Ludwig Wittgenstein*, p. 58.

M.32   81 East Rd
                                          Monday
                                          [4 or 11 January 1937]

DEAR MOORE,

I could not leave Cambridge last week as I wished. Instead I had
to go to bed on Wednesday with a 'flu. I'm out of bed again but
still *very* weak. Do you think you could come and have tea with
me here tomorrow? – But on second thought I find that I shall be
absolutely well enough to come to you. So I'll come to you at
about 5 p.m., unless I hear from you to the contrary. I *very* much
want to speak to you.

                              Yours

                                   LUDWIG WITTGENSTEIN

M.33   Tuesday
                                [5 or 12 January 1937)

DEAR MOORE,

   I'm sorry I didn't come to you today but I didn't feel quite well enough for it. Mrs Moore wrote to me that you too were having 'flu. I hope it was only a light attack. With me a 'flu, however short, has a long epilogue. And I'm just in the beginning of it. When I shall be well enough I'll come round and try to see you, for I'm sure you'd better stay at home for several days.

Yours

LUDWIG WITTGENSTEIN

M.34   Skjolden i Sogn
                                        Thursday 4.3.[1937]

DEAR MOORE,

This is only to say that I wish to hear from you. – My work hasn't been going well since I came back here. Partly because I've been troubled about myself a lot. In the last few days I've been able to work a bit better, but still only very moderately. The days are getting longer now and that cheers me up, but I still don't see the sun from where I live. (Though in the village it shines for many hours.)

Give my love to Wisdom and tell him, please, to write to me occasionally. Have you heard from Rhees? I suppose you haven't seen Skinner, or I would have heard it from him. Though I wish you had! –

I enclose two stamps which might be of use to Mrs Moore. Please remember me to her. I hope to hear from you soon.

Lots of good wishes!

                         Yours

                              LUDWIG WITTGENSTEIN

M.37   81 East Rd.
                                                          Cambridge
                                                          19.10.38.

DEAR MOORE,

I am still not at all well. I am bodily very weak and shaky, and feel incapable of thinking properly about any subject. I cannot therefore start lecturing now, and I don't know whether I shall regain sufficient strength in the next 3 weeks, say, to do so. What the cause of my condition is I don't know for certain, but I believe it is the recent 'flu and the great nervous strain of the last month or two. (My people in Vienna are in great trouble.)

I wonder whether it had not better be announced in the Reporter that I can't lecture for the present and until further notice.

Would you mind letting me know what you think best, or just *do* what you think best?

Good wishes.

Yours

LUDWIG WITTGENSTEIN

My people in Vienna. – After the Nazi invasion of Austria in March 1938, Wittgenstein's three sisters and other members of his family who lived in Austria were in considerable danger because of their Jewish ancestry. It was the *Anschluß* which prompted Wittgenstein to apply for British citizenship.

M.38   81 East Rd.
                                                   20.10.38.

DEAR MOORE,

I had a note from Ewing today saying that I have been appointed a member of the Mor[al] Sc[ience] faculty. Could you
tell me what exactly this means? Didn't I belong to the faculty
before, and what has changed, now I do belong to it? Do I have
new duties, or new rights? If you would let me have a line explaining this I should be grateful. Good wishes!

                              Yours

                      LUDWIG WITTGENSTEIN

P.S. I have seen the program of the Mor[al] Sc[iences] Cl[ub]. I
think it's *awful*.

Moral Science Faculty. – The traditional name of what is, since 1969,
called the Faculty of Philosophy at Cambridge.

M.40   81, East Rd.
                                                                              Cambridge
                                                                              2.2.39.

DEAR MOORE,

I had a p[ost] c[ard] on Wednesday from Keynes saying that he
would like to see the English version of my book, or whatever is
ready of it. I needn't say the whole thing is absurd as he couldn't
even make head or tail of it if it were translated very well. But as a
matter of fact the translation is pretty awful as I saw today when I
tried to go through it in order to correct it before giving it to
Keynes. Though I worked quite hard on it the whole day with
Smythies we only did 12 pages, because masses of it had to be
altered. Tomorrow I must go on with it because tomorrow night
Keynes ought to get it. So I'm afraid I shan't be able to come to
you in the afternoon. I have written to Keynes that you have read
the first half of my first volume and could give him some information about it; for obviously you must be able to get more out of
reading the original than Keynes could get out of a bad translation *and in a hurry*. So I *hope* he'll ask you to give him your opinion.
By the way, please don't mention to *anyone* that I don't think
highly of the translation. Rhees did his very best and the stuff is
damn difficult to translate.

   I hope to see you soon. Best wishes!

                                        Yours

                                              LUDWIG WITTGENSTEIN

Cf. K.28–30.

M.42   Trinity Coll[ege]
                                                       Friday
                                                       [October 1944]

DEAR MOORE,

I should like to tell you how glad I am that you read us a paper
yesterday. It seems to me that the most important point was the
"absurdity" of the assertion "There is a fire in this room and I
don't believe there is." To call this, as I think you did, "an absurdity for *psychological* reasons" seems to me to be wrong, or *highly*
misleading. (If I ask someone "Is there a fire in the next room?"
and he answers "I believe there is" I can't say: "Don't be irrelevant. I asked you about the fire, not about your state of mind!")
But what I wanted to say was this. Pointing out that "absurdity"
which is in fact something *similar* to a contradiction, though it
isn't one, is so important that I *hope you'll publish* your paper. By
the way, don't be shocked at my saying it's something "similar"
to a contradiction. This means roughly: it plays a similar role in
logic. You have said something about the *logic* of assertion. Viz.:
It makes sense to say "Let's suppose: p is the case and I don't believe that p is the case", whereas it makes *no* sense to assert "⊢p is
the case and I don't believe that p is the case". This *assertion* has to
be ruled out and *is* ruled out by "common sense", just as a contradiction is. And this just shows that logic isn't as simple as logi-
cians think it is. In particular: that contradiction isn't the *unique*
thing people think it is. It isn't the *only* logically inadmissible form
and it is, under certain circumstances, admissible. And to show
this seems to me the chief merit of your paper. In a word it seems
to me that you've made a *discovery*, and that you should publish it.

I hope to see you privately some day.

                                                 Yours sincerely
                                                 L. WITTGENSTEIN

Dated by Moore.
I have not been able to identify the paper which Moore gave to the
Moral Sciences Club in October 1944. The first writer, to my know-

ledge, who drew attention to the puzzle about saying and disbelieving which has become known as "Moore's Paradox", was A. M. MacIver in a paper "Some Questions about 'Know' and 'Think'" in *Analysis 5*, 1937–1938. Moore refers to the puzzle in several of his writings from the war years: in "A Reply to my Critics" in *The Philosophy of G. E. Moore*, ed. by P. Schilpp, Evanston 1942, p. 543, in "Russell's 'Theory of Descriptions'" in *The Philosophy of Bertrand Russell*, ed. by P. Schilpp, Evanston 1944, p. 204, and in "Four Forms of Scepticism", which was delivered as a lecture to various universities during Moore's stay in the United States in the period 1940–1944 and was published in *Philosophical Papers*, London 1959. I am not aware of any writing by Moore which dealt exclusively with the paradox.

M.43   Trin[ity] Coll[ege]
                                                Monday
                                                [November 1944]

DEAR MOORE,

I was sorry to hear in the Moral Sc[iences] Club on Saturday that you were resigning your Chairmanship. It wasn't really necessary to resign it as I could always have deputized for you, whenever you didn't feel inclined or able to come. – I was, as you can imagine, elected chairman, after your letter had been read to the Club. I *hope* this doesn't mean that you aren't going to come to the meetings when your health will again permit it (and some moderately interesting person reads a paper). I should very much like to see you before long if it's all right with you.

Yours

L. WITTGENSTEIN

Dated by Moore.

M.44   [Date unknown]

DEAR MOORE,

This copy is lousy, but it's all I can get. Probably you have the "Studien" already, then just throw these away. My favourites are No 4 and 5.

5 must be played very *crisply* and with a *serious* expression, *not* as though it were meant, in some way, to be witty.

Yours

L. WITTGENSTEIN

P.S. The marmalade is grand and not at all *bitter*.

The date of this letter is not known but there is some evidence that it belongs in this place in the series.

Mr Timothy Moore informs me that the pieces of music for the piano referred to probably were Schumann's "Studien für den Pedal-Flügel", Op. 56.

M.45   Trinity Coll[ege]
                                           Sunday
                                           22 July 1945

DEAR MOORE,

I'm sorry I can't come on Tuesday, but I can and shall on Friday, and I'm looking forward to it. – Looking through a copy of the stuff I gave you I see that there are a good many *nasty* misprints, *i.e.* such as suggest a wrong sense. If I have an opportunity I'll correct them.

                              Yours

                                    L. WITTGENSTEIN

Dated by Moore.

stuff I gave you. – Refers presumably to a collection of remarks (*Bemerkungen I*) which Wittgenstein used for the final version of the first part of the *Investigations*.

M.46   Trin[ity] Coll[ege]
                                                     Tuesday
                                                     [7(?) August 1945]

DEAR MOORE,

Thanks for your letter. I'm sorry I shan't hear the Bruckner
now. Poor Tim! – I think I understand your remark about the
Schubert and I feel something I could express in the same words.
I believe it's something like this, that the Quintet has a *fantastic*
kind of greatness. Is this what you'd say? By the way, it was
played *by far* better than I had expected.

                    So long! Good wishes!
                              Yours

                                   L. WITTGENSTEIN

This is a reply to a letter from Moore to Wittgenstein dated 5 August
1945 which has been preserved. Moore and his son Timothy played
duets on the piano and Wittgenstein was present as a listener. The plan
had been to play an arrangement for the piano of Bruckner's seventh
symphony, but the occasion had to be cancelled because of overtime
work which Timothy Moore (Tim) had to do. The reference to Schubert is to the Quintet in C major, op. 163, which Wittgenstein thought
one of the greatest of musical works.

M.47   Trinity College
                                            Cambridge
                                            Thursday
                                            [Probably October 1946]

DEAR MOORE,

I was sorry I was not allowed to see you today. Mrs Moore
wrote to me, could I come next Tuesday, instead. Now I'm free
on Tuesday afternoon and, as you know, should like to see you,
not for any particular reason, but in an ordinary friendly way. But
I am sure you'll understand that, – under the peculiar circumstances, – I should like to know whether what Mrs Moore wrote
to me was an honest to God invitation for me to come and see you
on Tuesday, or whether it was a kind of hint that I'd better not
try to see you. If it was the latter, please don't hesitate to say so. I
will not be hurt *in the slightest*, for I know that queer things happen in this world. It's one of the few things I've really learnt in my
life. So please, if that's how it is, just write on a p[ost] c[ard]
something like "Don't come". I enclose a card in case you haven't
got one. I'll understand everything. Good luck and good wishes!

                          Yours

                                    LUDWIG WITTGENSTEIN

M.49   Trin[ity] Coll[ege]
                                                Camb[ridge]
                                                14.11.46.

DEAR MOORE,

I don't believe for a moment that you'll want to come to the
Moral Sc[iences] Club tonight (I'm giving a talk, roughly, on
what I believe philosophy is, or what the method of philosophy
is) – but I want to say that if you *should* turn up for the paper, or
the discussion, the club, and particularly I, would be *honoured*.

                                Yours sincerely

                                L. WITTGENSTEIN

Trinity College
Cambridge.
3.12.46.

Dear Moore,

As far as I can see
now I will be in
London on Thursday
afternoon. & unable
to see you. Would it
be all right if I called
on you (in case I
were here after all?
If you're otherwise
engaged then, it doesn't
matter & I'll just go away.
If, as is most likely,
I shan't be back on
Thursday afternoon,
could I see you
Thursday week? — Price

M.51   Trinity College
                                                         Cambridge
                                                         3.12.46.

DEAR MOORE,

As far as I can see now I will be in London on Thursday afternoon and unable to see you. Would it be all right if I called on you
in case I were here after all? If you're otherwise engaged then, it
doesn't matter and I'll just go again. If, as is most likely, I shan't
be back on Thursday afternoon, could I see you Thursday week?
– Price at the last Mor[al] Sc[iences] Cl[ub] meeting was *by far*
better than Austin had been. Price was willing to discuss important points. Unfortunately (I believe) Russell was there and most
disagreeable. Glib and superficial, though, as always, *astonishingly*
quick. I left at about 10.30 and felt exceedingly happy when I was
out in the street and away from the atmosphere of the M[oral]
Sc[iences] Cl[ub].

                         So long!
                                 Yours

                                         L. WITTGENSTEIN

M.53   [Trinity College, Cambridge]
                                   18.2.47.

DEAR MOORE,

I think I'd better not come and see you this Thursday. I'm in good health, but teaching philosophy almost every day seems to exhaust me a good deal and it might be better if I avoid a serious talk on Thursday. You know, of course, I'd *like* to come, for I enjoy talking with you, and I don't really know if it's worth saving my strength for teaching people most of whom can't learn anything anyway. If you let me I'll come to you next week or the week after.

Yours ever

LUDWIG WITTGENSTEIN

M.55   [Trinity College, Cambridge]
                                Sunday
                                [November 1947]

DEAR MOORE,

   This is only to say that I've found the missing M.S.S. Miss Anscombe had not just *one* copy, as I believed, and I found part of a
M.S. in my own possession, and together and with the bit you
have the three copies are complete. I needn't say I'm glad.

   I also wish to say that I enjoyed VERY much seeing you these
last 5 weeks. I think, in a way, more than I used to. I wish you lots
of good luck!

                            Yours

                                L. WITTGENSTEIN

P.S. I shall give Drury your good wishes. You didn't actually tell
me to, but I know it's all right with you.

   Dated by Moore.

   M.S.S. – Refers to the typescript of the first part of the *Investigations*.

   In October 1947 Wittgenstein had resigned the professorship. The
resignation became effective from 31 December. The Michaelmas Term
he spent at Cambridge on a ("sabbatical") leave of absence.

M.56   Ross's Hotel
                                              Parkgate Street
                                              Dublin, Eire
                                              16.12.48.

DEAR MOORE,

The enclosed card is to wish you as much happiness and as little unhappiness as possible. But I'm also writing you this note: for two reasons. I had a letter and Christmas card from Malcolm, and he says that he hasn't yet heard from you. When I read this I thought of your telling me that you'd write to him; that was in October in your room when I mentioned the fact that he had complained to me about not hearing from you. And at the same time I thought of something else you promised me then, i.e., putting it into your will that my typescripts, now in your possession, should, after your death, go to my executors, or to me if I should then be alive. – This letter is to remind you of both matters, in case you have forgotten. You are in a position to give a *great* deal of pleasure (in the first case) and to avert a *great* deal of distress (in the second) by comparatively simple means.

Rhees is coming here for 10 days next week. I am well and working pretty hard. May you be well, too!

Forgive me this lengthy letter.

                                        Yours

                                        LUDWIG WITTGENSTEIN

P.S. I know it's a lot to ask it – but if you could write me a line I'd be *very* glad. The above address is my address.

typescripts. – At the death of Wittgenstein in 1951 Moore had in his possession only the typescript of the *Philosophische Bemerkungen* which Wittgenstein had given him some time in the 1930's. Moore shortly after gave it to Wittgenstein's Literary Executors.

M.57
                                        Ross's Hotel
                                        Parkgate Street
                                        Dublin
                                        31.12.48.

DEAR MOORE,

Thanks for your letter and for having fulfilled both promises. My executors are *Rhees* and *Burnaby of Trinity*.

I wish you all good luck!

                              Yours

                              L. WITTGENSTEIN

Rhees leaves me tomorrow. He sends his love and respects, and so does Drury. I can still work fairly well though not as I did a month ago.

Burnaby. – The Rev. John Burnaby, b. 1891, Fellow of Trinity College, lecturer and later Regius Professor of Divinity at Cambridge.

In his final will, dated Oxford 29 January 1951, Wittgenstein appointed Rhees alone as his executor and Anscombe, Rhees, and von Wright as his Literary Executors.